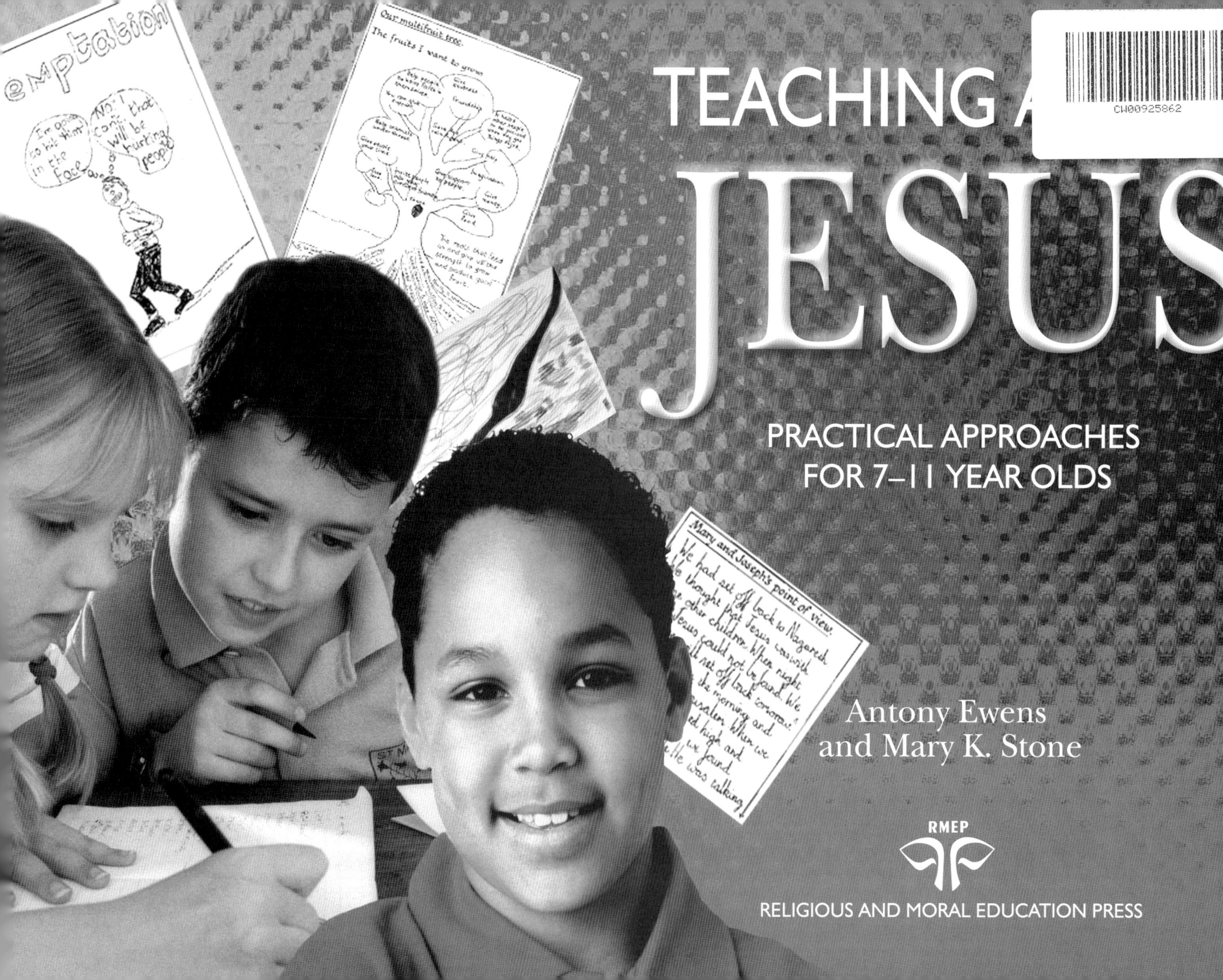

TEACHING A

JESUS

PRACTICAL APPROACHES FOR 7–11 YEAR OLDS

Antony Ewens
and Mary K. Stone

RMEP
RELIGIOUS AND MORAL EDUCATION PRESS

Religious and Moral Education Press
A division of SCM-Canterbury Press Ltd
A wholly owned subsidiary of Hymns Ancient & Modern Ltd
St Mary's Works, St Mary's Plain
Norwich, Norfolk NR3 3BH

First published 2001

ISBN 1 85175 223 4

About the Authors

Mary Stone and Tony Ewens teach RE at St Martin's College, Lancaster, where they have contributed to both pre-service and in-service courses. They are both experienced primary-school teachers who have held headships and been RE co-ordinators, and both have worked as advisory teachers for RE, in Cumbria and Devon respectively.

Acknowledgements

We should like to acknowledge our gratitude to the following who have helped us in a variety of ways in the preparation of this book:

Staff and pupils of Sedbergh Primary School, Cumbria, and especially Jan McArthur, the governors of Hornby CE Primary School, Lancashire and Oldham LEAs.

Scriptures quoted from the *Good News Bible* published by The Bible Societies/HarperCollins Publishers Ltd UK are © American Bible Society, 1966, 1971, 1976, 1992.

Designed and typeset by TOPICS – The Creative Partnership, Exeter
Illustrations mostly come from Sedbergh Primary School
Cover photographs: Digital Imagery © copyright 2001 Photodisc, Inc.
Printed in Great Britain by David Gregson Associates, Beccles, Sulfolk, for SCM-Canterbury Press Ltd, Norwich.

Preface

We have written this book in order to share with other teachers some practical ideas on RE with pupils in the 7–11 age group. The approaches that we describe have been used in classrooms, with positive results for children's motivation and learning. They spring from a determination to link children's growing knowledge about religion with developing their ability to reflect on their own ideas, opinions and beliefs.

Above all, this material is designed to be a source of ideas. We hope that teachers will draw on our examples by amending and adapting them to suit the needs of their pupils. The content and the methods which we describe are congruent with current statutory syllabuses for RE.

At the beginning of each piece of work an age range is given. This indicates the ages of the particular group of children whose responses are included in that example. It does not mean that the topic is suitable only for that age group. Many of these examples can be adapted to suit any children aged between 7 and 11 years, or indeed, older children, and the same basic content has been used with adults as well, e.g. with teachers on in-service courses.

Contents

Introduction

Examples of Units of Work

The Starting-Point

Every subject in the primary school curriculum has changed significantly in the last half century, but perhaps none more so than Religious Education. Differences in the religious, cultural and moral make-up of the community and a profound change in attitude towards the place of religion in society have brought about a re-evaluation of the place and scope of RE as an educational activity. This has been widely debated in journals and its implications have been extensively considered by each Local Education Authority (LEA) in England and Wales as it has written and reviewed its Agreed Syllabus for RE. However, as OFSTED reports often demonstrate, the practical applications of the change in thinking about RE have been slow to percolate into classrooms. This is hardly surprising, given the phenomenal demands made upon primary teachers by a constantly evolving national curriculum, the national literacy and numeracy strategies, statutory assessment, recording and reporting of pupils' attainment and the rapid development of new technology. RE is but one demand among many.

Despite official encouragement to introduce more subject-specialist teaching for ages 7–11, most primary practioners are still predominantly class teachers, attempting to provide the full range of a broad and balanced curriculum for their classes. In RE this is a mixed blessing. On one hand it means that children are tackling RE with a teacher who will know each of them very well, and this can be a major benefit to their spiritual, moral, social and cultural development. On the other hand the majority of primary teachers have only a limited knowledge of the key features of the principal faiths covered in contemporary syllabuses. Many of them will have experienced RE in their own schooldays restricted to the telling and learning of biblical stories, and the few hours devoted to RE in their teacher training will have done little to equip them with more than a sketchy outline of the subject knowledge which seems to be taken for granted by today's syllabus makers.

Getting Started

It is our view that the most important task in RE at ages 7–11 is to help pupils to forge a link between their own spiritual development and the ideas, practices and teachings of the faiths about which they learn. By pupils' spiritual development we mean their capacity to reflect on what it means to be a human being, with emotions and insights as well as thoughts and knowledge, and their ability to explore big questions about the origins, purpose and end of life, the nature of human relationships and the relationship between human beings and their environment. These issues form a key part of the agendas of each of the principal religions. By encountering examples of the ways in which some people have answered – and continue to answer – the big questions about human existence, children can be helped to shape and formulate their own responses and views.

In order to bring this aspiration to life in the primary classroom, teachers of RE need:

- to see RE as open and exploratory, and be willing to explore their own beliefs and values;
- to view their own role as that of educator rather than instructor;
- to help children to engage in a quest for meaning and purpose in life.

What follows in this book is founded on these principles.

A Practical Approach to Religious Education

In our work with teachers, on both pre-service and in-service courses, the commonest request that we receive is:

Give us some practical ideas for RE that we can use in the classroom.

We are happy to oblige (see pages 16–45). But even the best of practical ideas depends to some extent for its success upon the teacher's knowledge and understanding of the subject-matter and appreciation of the aims and purposes of the subject. No amount of practical advice can equip you to handle the unexpected, spontaneous question from a pupil or parent (or, perish the thought, OFSTED inspector).

- So our first practical advice is that there is no substitute for thinking through your understanding of the role of RE in the school curriculum.
- Our second suggestion is that you should develop gradually your knowledge of the religions covered in the syllabus that you are required to teach.
- A third recommendation is that you review the range of teaching and learning styles that you use in RE.

However, we do not hold to the view that you need a full grasp of theory before you can begin with practice. The relationship between practice and theory is much more complex than that. We have both developed much of our theoretical understanding of RE through reflecting on our work in classrooms, in primary schools and in pre-service and in-service work with teachers in a college and for several LEAs. We also acknowledge our indebtedness to many authors of books about RE. But we have derived the greatest benefit from books and journals through having already tackled aspects of the subject in a practical way. We find ourselves recognizing the ideas and issues dealt with in the literature because we have already encountered them in the classroom. The writers then help us to evaluate our practice, to build on the strengths and eliminate the weaknesses. Our recommended approach is precisely the same as that followed by Early Years pupils whose teachers use the High/Scope method:

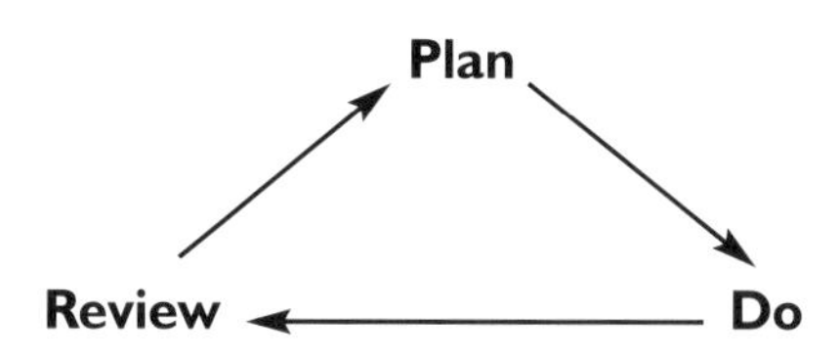

Constant use of this cycle leads to the ongoing development and refinement of a theoretical approach to RE by a process of reflection on practice. But your theories never become divorced from reality because they immediately feed back into the classroom through your next plans.

The most important stage of the cycle is the review. This may comprise some or all of the following:

- evaluation – of processes and/or outcomes;
- reflection – on what has been achieved, and what might follow;
- discussion – with colleagues and/or pupils;
- reading – RE scheme or syllabus, journal or books.

However, you cannot review an RE lesson until you have taught one. The activities in this book are designed as 'starters', to be used with or without adaptation, to get you under way in the cycle of Plan–Do–Review.

This is emphatically **not** a volume of ideas to be used unthinkingly. We encourage you to modify and amend our work, in particular to meet the needs of the children you teach. Above all, we want to offer as starting-points ideas that have been tried out in classrooms, and which worked. They are presented as a means to an end: as launching-pads to provide teachers with the confidence to develop their own repertoire of approaches through engaging in the cycle of Plan–Do–Review which we have found so beneficial.

The Questions People Ask

This section deals with some of the questions that class teachers in England and Wales most frequently ask us about RE. We mention them here for two reasons:

- to provide some answers;
- to equip RE co-ordinators who will no doubt encounter the same questions.

Is RE in the National Curriculum?

Yes and no! RE is part of the basic curriculum, required by law to be taught in all maintained schools in England and Wales. The Dearing Review of the National Curriculum recommended that it be allocated at least 45 hours per year at Key Stage 2 and 36 hours at Key Stage 1. When the Labour government lifted the requirement to teach the full programmes of study in the foundation subjects (Art, Design & Technology, Geography, History, Music and PE), the Secretary of State made it clear that no reduction in RE was permitted. RE is therefore classified as one of the core subjects, along with English, Mathematics, Science and ICT, and OFSTED has instructed its inspectors to inspect it as such. However, there is no national programme of study for RE. The QCA programmes of study show possible ways of planning schemes of work, though teachers will need to be careful that any adopted fulfil the requirements of their own Agreed Syllabus. The QCA *Non-statutory guidance on RE* (ref. QCA/00/576) is an excellent guide to all planning.

Why is there no national programme of study for RE?

Two main reasons: first, before the National Curriculum came in there was already a procedure in place for agreeing syllabuses for RE, and this has continued, and secondly, the dual system of schools includes denominational schools, some of which have the authority to give religious education in accordance with the faith to which they belong.

How do I know which syllabus to use?

Community schools and almost all foundation schools use the agreed syllabus of their LEA. This is agreed by the LEA on the advice of a conference (called a SACRE) including representatives of the Church of England, other Christian denominations, other principal faiths with a significant local presence, the teaching profession and elected councillors. It must be non-denominational in character and must reflect the major role of Christianity within national culture but also require teaching about the other principal faiths practised in Britain (defined usually as Buddhism, Hinduism, Islam, Judaism and Sikhism).

Almost all aided schools have a denominational character (Church of England and Roman Catholic are the most numerous, and there are also Methodist, Jewish and Islamic schools). The governors of these schools are responsible for ensuring that the character of RE is in accordance with the traditions of their foundation. In practice the governors usually adopt a syllabus proposed by their religious authorities. Teaching about that particular religious tradition will be prominent, but most syllabuses used in aided schools also require teaching about other faiths and denominations.

In most schools the RE co-ordinator will have led the drawing up of a scheme of work which is in line with the syllabus, so other teachers should not have to become very closely involved with the syllabus itself.

Why teach RE in schools?
Surely we should educate, not indoctrinate?

With respect, you've answered your own question. Indoctrination (promoting one point of view as if there were no other) is specifically ruled out in legislation. In the syllabuses of LEAs and religious authorities alike the RE teacher is seen an educator, who helps children to explore a range of religious practices, beliefs and customs and a variety of human experiences. Against this backdrop it is for parents to arrange for their children's nurture within a religion if they wish.

What's the point of RE?

The School Curriculum and Assessment Authority (SCAA) produced in 1994 some Model Syllabuses for RE, and these have been re-issued by its successor body, the Qualifications and Curriculum Authority (QCA). These syllabuses are not addressed to schools. They are principally provided for LEAs, to guide them in making their agreed syllabuses.

The Model Syllabuses propose two attainment targets:

AT1 – Learning about religions
AT2 – Learning from religion

Many LEAs have incorporated these into their syllabuses. In others, even if they have not done so, it is possible to trace two separate strands within their documents, and we find these ATs useful in helping to achieve and maintain balance in a programme of RE.

AT1 ('Learning *about* religions') sets out to give children an understanding of the main practices and beliefs of the principal faiths. Given the continuing prevalence among primary teachers of the notion that concrete experiences logically precede abstract thought, it may help if you pose the question in this way:

What do Christians (or Muslims, or Jews, etc.) do and why do they do it?

Most RE syllabuses ask you to teach about a range of practices (such as worship, lifestyle, festivals, initiation ceremonies and the roles of special places and people) in Christianity and two other faiths at ages 7–11. A wider range of topics and religions is covered at ages 11–14. A secure grasp of this information and a developing understanding of the role of the various religious practices in each of the faiths is very valuable for children growing up in a plural society.

AT2 ('Learning *from* religion') seeks to enable children to explore their own experiences of life and to wrestle with key spiritual and moral questions: How did life begin? How will it end? Does it have a purpose or do we have to create our own meanings? How should we behave towards other people, the natural world and ourselves? Why is there suffering? What qualities and values should we admire, and which deplore? Such questions are not confined to RE; they may occur in the study of literature or science, for example. However, AT2 is always an integral part of RE. If you remove it, you are left with a 'Cook's Tour' of faiths, relying solely upon children learning and regurgitating facts about religions. Highlight AT2, however, and you engage children in the most fascinating study of all: the study of who we are and what we might be and do.

Getting to Grips with an RE Syllabus

This section is about extending your skills as an RE teacher by enhancing your understanding of the aims of the subject and thinking through the main implications of the demands of a typical RE syllabus.

Many syllabuses are based overtly on the attainment targets from the SCAA/QCA Model Syllabuses:

AT1 – Learning about religions
AT2 – Learning from religion

Even where this is not the case, the influence of these aspects of RE can be detected in almost all syllabuses, whether provided by LEAs or by religious authorities, in Scotland and Ireland, as well as England and Wales.

In this book we have used these two ATs to provide suggestions for learning outcomes for each of the units of work (pages 16–45). We have described them as Possible Learning Outcomes to emphasize that our ideas are open to amendment to suit the needs of particular contexts.

AT1 – Learning *about* religions

Most syllabuses describe areas of content that should be covered, arranged in a Programme of Study for each Key Stage (or even, sometimes, each year group). This content can provide a good range of general knowledge about the religions studied, and this is useful. Any teacher, however apprehensive about RE, can feel secure in dealing with factual information: Sunday is a special day for Christians, Muslims face Makkah when they pray, Jews observe the Passover each year, and so on. But if AT1 is left at that point, it is little more than a 'Trivial Pursuits' exercise in gathering snippets of information. The question 'Why?' springs readily to the lips of children aged 7–11, and in our experience the most fruitful learning in RE has often occurred when we have allowed, and even encouraged, children to pursue their 'Why?'questions.

Why is Sunday a special day for Christians?

Why do Muslims face Makkah when they pray?

Why do Jews observe the Passover each year?

'Why?' is the question which points people beyond superficial knowledge towards a depth of understanding. In answering 'Why?' questions we place fragments of information into structured patterns of thinking which help us to make sense of the subject-matter.

'Why?' is also the question which arises out of curiosity and puzzlement. It is often a sign that the child who asks it has a keen motivation and interest in the topic, surely a strong enough reason to train children to adopt a questioning attitude to their learning. But 'Why?' is also the question which makes teachers of RE anxious:

What if I don't know the answer? …

What if I misrepresent the deeply held beliefs of a faith community? …

What if I don't believe it myself? …

And it is the 'Why?' question which consequently persuades many teachers to play safe and stick to the teaching and learning of the purely factual in RE.

Here are several pertinent points that we hope will encourage you or your colleagues not to shy away from the 'Why?' questions in RE:

- There is a close connection between the 'Why' questions in AT1 in RE and the central thrust of AT1 in both Mathematics and Science. In these subjects, too, teachers are frequently less confident with open-ended, exploratory work. Inspectors often remark that mathematical investigations and scientific hypotheses and experiments are done less well than areas of Maths and Science with clear right/wrong answers. Teachers' diffidence is not due simply to the fact that RE is somehow 'different'. It has more to do with an understandable apprehension about launching into any work which cannot be planned in detail.
- The ability to sort and classify information and to place it in a structured pattern enables learners to see meaningful

relationships between different bits of knowledge, rather like creating a picture out of the pieces of a jigsaw. So pursuing 'Why?' questions in RE is vitally important if children are to gain a coherent view of Christianity and other religions.

- The teacher need not be the repository of all knowledge and understanding. While we don't subscribe to the 'go away and find out' response to children's awkward questions, we do believe that it is a healthy sign for teachers to reveal the limits of their own knowledge, and to express an interest in finding out what they don't know. The search for answers to 'Why?' questions readily creates realistic opportunities to use and extend higher-order English skills, whether in reading texts or electronically accessed data, or questioning a visitor from a faith community or 'interrogating' a photograph or poster.
- It is useful for children to hypothesize in RE, just as in Science. 'I wonder how many possible reasons we can think of' is a valuable precursor to some research, and children's suggestions may well provide clues as to the nature and quality of their thinking.
- Because of the diversity within religions, there may well be different 'right' answers to 'Why?' questions. Ask six Christians why they attend church and they may produce six different answers. Learning to accept and appreciate a diversity of views and beliefs is a valuable component of preparation for life in a plural society.
- If the teacher is a co-learner with the class, s/he can model appropriate attitudes of curiosity, interest, appreciation and respect, and ceases to be an apparent spokesperson for the faith being studied. S/he therefore protects the integrity of any personal religious standpoint and deals with the subject-matter in a thoroughly educational way. The use of well-briefed visitors who do represent the religions covered by the syllabus is thus doubly helpful, providing authentic data and confirming the teacher in an educator's role.

With regard to AT1 our view is, therefore, that you cannot learn about religions just by collecting factual information about them. 'What do Christians do?' is a valuable starting-point, enabling children to learn about worship, prayer, the use of the Bible, lifestyle, festivals, customs and much more. 'Why do they do it?' opens the way for an exploration of the beliefs and insights which underpin the outward manifestations of Christian practice. The same principle applies to other faiths.

AT2 – Learning *from* religion

As well as promoting knowledge and understanding of the principal faiths, RE is designed to assist children to formulate their own opinions and beliefs. 'Learning from religion' can be viewed in various ways. We consider it helpful to link this attainment target with the notions of spiritual, moral and social and cultural (SMSC) development, areas made familiar in schools in England and Wales by their inclusion in the OFSTED inspection schedule and in the QCA *Non-statutory guidance on RE* (ref. QCA/00/576).

The **spiritual** category includes feelings and insights about the purpose and meaning of life, a sense of mystery and wonder about the natural world, and ideas and beliefs about the existence of a God or gods. The approaches to RE which we describe below encourage children to pose and investigate questions of this kind and we find that the way in which we teach leads almost automatically to this sort of questioning.

Many of the issues encountered in RE also have implications about right and wrong, and lead into discussions of ethical principles and principled behaviour, thus fostering **moral** development. Often the issues raised are about the interrelationships among people within groups to which they belong, providing material for **social** development. Opportunities to promote **cultural** development are also plentiful: children can learn from religion about the way in which religious beliefs influence lifestyles, customs and traditions. They can also be encouraged to adopt a positive, appreciative attitude towards diversity.

The most profitable work in AT2 comes as a result of enabling children to explore their own responses to the aspects of religion being studied and to relate these to their own life experiences. This calls for specific skills and attitudes on the part of the teacher, chief among which are:

- an ability to frame genuinely open questions to promote enquiry;
- the use of phraseology which encourages reflection and an individual response (e.g. 'I wonder why …?');
- being prepared to accept and work with unexpected responses.

Current professional practice in primary education accentuates the importance of thorough planning by the teacher. Important though this is, there is a sense in which tight planning can stifle attainment in this area of RE. We suggest that teachers should take great care with the preparation of questions and other prompts which will promote reflection and deep thought. Thereafter they need to be ready to respond positively and productively to whatever children say. We have deliberately included in our examples extracts from conversations between teachers and pupils to illustrate ways of doing this – and to show the variety and depth of thinking which it is possible to stimulate in children aged 7–11.

Planning Units of Work

In responding to the main aims of RE set out in a syllabus, our usual practice when planning has been the following:

1. Identify the aspect of the programme of study which we intend to cover.
2. Clarify the intended learning outcomes in terms of AT1, i.e. what do we intend children to learn *about* religion?
3. Consider the possibilities offered by this topic for AT2, i.e. what might children learn *from* this area of religion?
4. Find an aspect of children's existing experience to use as a bridge between themselves and the material to be studied, e.g. work about a sacred text might begin or end with consideration of a book which is special to the pupil.

In this way we can ensure that our planning is rooted in the subject-matter set out in the syllabus and also that it relates to children's existing understanding.

How to Achieve Progression and Continuity in RE

The notions of progression and continuity imply that children's learning should be ordered and sequenced, both in a logical way and in its practical implementation in school. These ideas are perhaps most easily illustrated in Mathematics, where concepts such as addition and subtraction recur at regular intervals, with steadily increasing complexity, in a pattern which fits Bruner's idea of a 'spiral curriculum'. In Bruner's work it is the key concepts or big ideas of a subject which are the building blocks for continuity and progression. This helps to explain why Maths is so easy to describe under this heading, since its key concepts are easily identified as addition, subtraction, area, volume, capacity and so on.

The equivalent terms in RE are less apparent, but a little detective work reveals categories such as worship, ritual, deity, celebration and revelation. Your RE syllabus will be structured in such a way as to build upon these key ideas, to deepen and extend children's knowledge and understanding of them and to reflect the developmental needs of learners in a sequenced programme of study. Teachers need to be aware of this process at work in the syllabus, and in the school's associated scheme of work for RE, in order to point children back to previous learning in the same area and forward to subsequent work. This helps to create for children something of the broad canvas, of which individual topics are but a small part.

Consider, for example, the extract below from the Agreed Syllabus (1996) of the Oldham LEA:

Learning about Religions				Learning from Religion		
Key Stage 3 [Ages 11–14]	**Key Stage 2 [Ages 7–11]**	**Key Stage 1 [Ages 5–7]**	**Core Objectives**	**Key Stage 1 [Ages 5–7]**	**Key Stage 2 [Ages 7–11]**	**Key Stage 3 [Ages 11–14]**
Children should learn about the initiation rites of the religions studied. So that they could, for example, describe the components of the initiation rites of the faiths studied, particularly those which convey the idea of commitment and responsibility.	Children should appreciate the significance of the elements in the birth rites of the religions studied. So that they could, for example, describe the components of the birth rites in the religions studied, and explain their significance.	Children should encounter the birth rite ceremonies in the religions studied. So that they could, for example, describe the main features of the ceremony in which young children are welcomed into a faith community.	**BELIEFS AND PRACTICES** Children will explore: • **belonging to a faith community**	Children should explore the sense of belonging to a community. So that they could, for example, talk about some of the groups to which they belong, or could belong, and what is good about them.	Children should develop an understanding of what it means to belong to a community. So that they could, for example, explain what benefits a particular community can give to an individual member, and what the individual would be expected to contribute in return.	Children should develop a sense of responsibility in relation to the immediate community. So that they could, for example, identify issues concerning the school, home, or neighbourhood, to which personal action can make a contribution.

The Oldham chart demonstrates clearly an appropriate progression in teaching and learning in respect of both children's developing understanding of entry into membership of a religion (AT1) and their appreciation of the qualities and characteristics of communities of various kinds, and the responsibilities of those who belong to them (AT2). In preparing a scheme of work and in planning RE lessons, RE co-ordinators and class teachers would need an awareness of the contribution made by an individual lesson or sequence of lessons to the overall development of the concepts of initiation rites, commitment, community and responsibility.

The Oldham example applies to a topic which may be dealt with only two or three times in a child's primary-school career. Some elements of RE recur more frequently than this, especially those connected with religious festivals, and particularly any which are marked in some way within the school, as is often the case with Christmas, for example.

We have deliberately omitted from this book a section about Christmas, since this festival is observed – often excessively, in our view – in most schools. We do, however, want to refer to Christmas in this section, since inspection evidence records that this topic is often characterized by repetition rather than progression, and that pupils aged 10–11 sometimes undertake similar tasks to those tackled in the reception class. We recommend to teachers the exercise undertaken by the staff of a primary school in East Lancashire, who used the Year Theme structure of the Lancashire Agreed Syllabus to devise a programme for their two-form entry school with the aim of stimulating a developing understanding of Christmas as a Christian festival. Their programme is reproduced below, but they would be the first to assert that there is no substitute for undertaking the process by means of which they discussed and agreed their plans.

CHRISTMAS THEMES
Developing Progression and Continuity

YEAR	THEME FROM LANCASHIRE SYLLABUS	SUGGESTIONS (It is assumed that children will encounter the Christmas Story each year, in assembly, plays and carols)
R [Ages 4–5]	Community	**Gifts** 1. Discussion of gifts we'd like to receive. 2. What gifts might we give? ... to whom? why? 3. Why do people give gifts (draw out ideas that (a) this marks special occasion (b) it shows they like/love someone) 4. When using Christmas Story, emphasise the point that Jesus' birth was announced as a gift … to Mary, to Shepherds … and that the Kings brought gifts. What would you have taken? … and why?
Year 1 [Ages 5–6]	God	**Births and Birthdays** 1. Discussion of the impact on a family of the arrival of a baby (practical issues and feelings, e.g. excitement, pride, jealousy). 2. What is your birthday (anniversary of your birth), how is it celebrated (bring in cards, presents, gather together for parties, sing Happy Birthday, special food, candles) 3. Why do people celebrate each other's birthdays? (Means, "you're important"). 4. When using Christmas Story, emphasise Christmas as the Christian celebration of Jesus' birthday. All the elements (cards, gifts, gatherings, food, singing [carols]) are present.
Year 2 [Ages 6–7]	Worship	**Good News** 1. Discussion of examples of good news in school or in papers/on TV. 2. How do people react to good news? (Applause, send someone a congratulations card, tell someone else about it.) 3. You could introduce the idea that sometimes people don't like hearing good news (e.g. jealous because someone else is praised). 4. When using Christmas Story, emphasise the giving of news (e.g. by the angels, and by the star, and [to Herod] by the wise men). How did people react? e.g. Shepherds, Kings went to see and take gifts. What about Herod? 5. Contemporary reactions to Christmas news: presents, parties, plays, carol singing.

Year 3 [Ages 7–8]	Founders and Leaders	**Changes** – One point about leaders is that they bring about changes in the lives of other people. 1. Focus on the characters in the Christmas Story whose lives were changed. Mary and Joseph, Shepherds, Wise Men (and Herod? – threatened by change). What were the changes? 2. Identify what would be different about life in Britain if Christmas did not exist – makes point that Jesus influences everyone not just Christians. 3. How did people in the Christmas Story show how they responded to Jesus as a "leader" (e.g. Shepherds worshipped; Wise Men gave gifts; Herod tried to kill him). 4. Does the Christmas Story help you to think about changes you want or ought to make in your life (link to New Year Resolution).
Year 4 [Ages 8–9]	Living the Faith	**Christmas Today** – Emphasis on how Christian Churches celebrate Christmas. You might visit one to find out or collect information sheets. 1. Types of services: carols, Blessing of Crib, Midnight Mass or Communion. 2. Read some of the Bible passages used in Churches (see Y5's unit for references). 3. Look at the words of some carols. How do they link up with Bible story? 4. Charitable work – collections of money and toys for Children's Society, shelter and food for the homeless (giving as important concept in Christianity, Jesus seen as "a gift"). 5. Study the Christingle ceremony, which links "giving" with the image of Jesus as "the light of the world".
Year 5 [Ages 9–10]	Sacred Books	**Read All About It** – Some parts of the Christmas Story are found in the Bible. Others parts are traditions, passed on orally. This unit focuses on research skill. The relevant passages are contained in Matthew chapters 1 and 2, Luke chapters 1 and 2. 1. Children give their own accounts of the Christmas Story (a list, not continuous prose). 2. Check the list against the Bible version. What's in the Bible? What's traditional? 3. Which incidents does Matthew include, but not Luke and vice versa? 4. Why do you think they give different accounts? (You could compare versions of a story in the *Daily Express* and *Daily Mirror* to give a modern illustration). 5. If time permits, investigate words of a carol. Do they come from the Bible account?
Year 6 [Age 10–11]	Life as a Journey	**Travellers** 1. Study in detail the story of the Three Wise Men (see Matthew chapter 2). 2. Get children to write "a Wise Man's Diary" (their traditional names were Caspar, Melchior, Balthasar), but give them a question for each stage of the journey (a) Do you really believe that stars give guidance? (b) Who or what were you expecting to find? (c) What did you feel about Herod? (d) Was your gift appropriate? 3. Discussion topics. These topics are about the children themselves, not in the Wise Man Role. (a) Who or what gives you guidance – are there good and bad influences? (b) What are you hoping to achieve in your life? (c) Who or what could help you/hinder you? (d) If you had taken a present to the baby Jesus, what would it be … and why?

Assessment, Recording and Reporting in RE

You can't assess RE. It's too personal.

That is a common response when we run courses on assessment in RE. We disagree. If RE is treated as an educational activity its outcomes should be as open to scrutiny as those of any other subject.

Reasons for Assessment

Consider this list produced by a group of final-year student teachers, although they don't claim to have said the last word on the subject!

- To find out what pupils know, understand and can do
- To help me decide where to begin in my teaching
- To enable me to give feedback to the children
- To help me to evaluate my teaching
- To inform me when I start to plan the next session
- To enable me to pitch activities more appropriately to children's abilities
- To provide evidence for writing reports
- To enable me to pass on information to the next teacher/school
- To provide material for me to record so that I have a sound basis of evidence to work with
- To give the children a chance to set targets for themselves and see how far they have been able to meet them
- To help me to work out why a child is having difficulties so that I can plan ways to help

It would be difficult to argue that any of these points is irrelevant to RE. Yet teachers often have a sense of unease about assessing in the subject, usually because of a feeling of trespassing into a child's insights and beliefs. The following extract from a school's RE policy reveals an approach which has been very carefully considered.

Extract from a School's RE Policy

ASSESSMENT, RECORDING AND REPORTING

Assessment incorporates observation of the processes involved, examination of the finished work and discussion with pupils. It is not the intention in RE to assess the pupils' beliefs or lack of them. It is, however, appropriate to judge the extent to which their understanding of religion is based upon accurate knowledge and developed skills. Assessment will also seek to identify their capacity for expressing opinions clearly and thoughtfully, for appreciating the opinions of others and for discussing differing points of view in a suitable manner.

Assessment takes place at the end of each topic. A record is kept of the work of each class on each topic. Notes will be kept of points of particular significance regarding the work of individuals, and important pieces of work will be considered for inclusion in children's assessment folders.

An overall comment on children's progress in RE will be included in the annual written report to parents.

This school has made a distinction between the two attainment targets. For AT1 ('Learning *about* religions'), it is clear that there is a body of knowledge that can readily be assessed: Jesus was born at Bethlehem, Jews worship in a synagogue, Muslims fast during Ramadan. Teachers can also consider children's understanding of such information. For AT2 ('Learning *from* religion') the issue is one not of assessing the beliefs and opinions that children hold, but of their ability to frame and articulate those insights and to consider thoughtfully the points of view of others. This is clearly assessable.

Is the workload manageable?

A pragmatic approach is taken by this school to the workload entailed in assessing RE – rightly so in our view. A strongly interactive approach to teaching RE, which we advocate, requires the teacher to 'be' with the class, participating fully in their learning experiences. This calls for an economical approach to paper-based assessment and for an attentive interest in the reactions and achievements of individual pupils during lessons; interactive teaching demands interactive assessment, not tick-sheet driven schedules. We propose the following documentation as adequate:

- **Written plans** for the work of the class showing long-term (annual scheme), medium-term (half-termly unit) and short-term (single lesson) intentions.
- Carefully drafted **learning outcomes** which 'cash-out' the relevant part of the programme of study, and demonstrate a balance between the two attainment targets (see, e.g., pages 7ff.).
- **Evaluation** after each unit including coverage of work, general assessment of the attainment of the class and notes of particular significance regarding individual pupils' progress.
- The **pupils' work**, marked promptly, with interactive feedback. For example, the teacher might pose a question for the child rather than making a closed comment.
- An **annual report to parents**, available to the next teacher, detailing the child's attainment in relation to the work covered. Appropriate comments can be drawn from the learning outcomes.

If you are fortunate, you will be working from a syllabus which provides much of the key information for you, as the examples below drawn from the Oldham Agreed Syllabus of 1996 show.

A teacher using this syllabus had taught a unit of work to her junior class about the parables of Jesus and was able to draw upon the learning outcomes (described under **'So that they could, for example'**) in her reports:

K_____ understands something of the importance of the parables of Jesus to Christians. He is able to explain some interpretations of the main parables and can relate them to his own experience.

Learning about Religions			Learning from Religion	
Key Stage 2 [Ages 7–11]	**Key Stage 1 [Ages 5–7]**	**Core Objectives**	**Key Stage 1 [Ages 5–7]**	**Key Stage 2 [Ages 7–11]**
Children should a. develop knowledge of holy books and other important religious literature.	**Children should** a. encounter some of the stories and other writings which are important to faith communities and begin to explore their meaning	**EXPRESSION** Children will explore: **Holy books, sacred writings, art, dance, music, drama, architecture and literature as means of expressing religious beliefs and feelings**	**Children should** a. enjoy stories from different traditions, and realise that stories from religious traditions often deal with concerns and feelings similar to their own	**Children should** a. talk about stories which focus on values, relationships or religious teachings and consider the relevance of this teaching for their own lives
So that they could, for example a. name the special writings which are important to faith communities studied; and describe some of their essential features. b. explain some of the interpretations of symbols, stories and language given by believers.	**So that they could, for example** a. remember the outline of stories they have heard and suggest why these stories are valued by the religious communities to which they belong.		**So that they could, for example** a. respond to the spiritual or religious aspects of stories in the light of their own experience and thoughts. b. draw on stimuli from the natural world in their creative work.	**So that they could, for example** a. describe some of the religious stories which teach us to care for each other and relate then to their own experience. b. draw on material which has arisen during times of stillness and reflection in their creative work.

From the Oldham Agreed Syllabus (1996)

Reflective Approaches Used in This Book

The methods we use are all-important if we wish the children:

- to find their work meaningful, whatever their faith position;
- to be able to reflect on motives, feelings and possible outcomes of courses of action;
- to be open and prepared to share their insights in a safe and supportive environment.

The methods suggested below are amply borne out in the practical examples that follow on pages 16–45:

Always start from children's own experience, and from what they know or think they know. Even as experienced teachers we can easily make false assumptions about children's knowledge. Brainstorming at the beginning of a lesson clarifies the starting-point. For example, during the first lesson of a series on the life of Jesus with 9–10 year olds the children were asked to brainstorm the word 'Jew'. The first three answers were:

> The little drops of water on the grass early in the morning.
>
> My mum said it before our Johnny was born. He's due any day now.
>
> Jesus was a Jew.

Before I could respond the rest of the class chorused:

> No, he wasn't!

How important it was for me to know this before continuing that first lesson!

Questions, well thought out, are crucial. The most important questions in life usually have more than one answer. They are generally about meaning and purpose in life; they are about beliefs and values, and children need to be challenged to grapple with the issues. We need to ask thought-provoking questions in such a way as to encourage the hesitant child. For example, 'I wonder why …?' is a good way to begin:

> ***I wonder why Jesus healed people?***
>
> ***I wonder how the disciples felt when they left Jesus to be arrested?***

There may be factual answers to these questions; nevertheless, it is better that the children have to think of possible answers for themselves. Given a chance children constantly surprise us.

> ***Did anything particularly surprise or interest you?***

This assumes a positive response, and more often than not creates a positive response from even the most reluctant child. Always give children the opportunity to ask questions. We don't have to know all the answers. There are ways of finding out: research using books, ask someone, use the Internet …

Take what the children say seriously and value it.
Try and find out the thinking that lies behind the question or statement.

Whenever possible give children a choice of activity.
Life is largely about making choices, so let's begin now. Providing a choice of activity removes the likelihood of a child saying they don't want to do something. For example, in the work on Zacchaeus (pages 21–24) the teacher gave the choice of writing a poem or expressing Zacchaeus' feelings in colour and form.

Ensure there's time for reflection and discussion whatever the main activity.
There is rarely time for every child to take part in a class discussion but sharing with a partner provides everyone with a chance to speak, and may well empower the more reticent child to share with the whole class.

Develop aspects of a topic that particularly interest the children.
Teachers plan with the children in mind, but there also need to be opportunities to follow up points that arise during the lesson.

Everyone in the class doesn't necessarily have to cover exactly the same work.
The children may be asked to research different aspects of the same topic, and then share their findings with the rest of the class. See the work on Resurrection (pages 35–38), where each pair of children read only one of the gospel accounts.

At all times we need to acknowledge the diversity of belief and practice within every religion.
It's important that we start by looking at the similarities, and only then explore the differences. It's not our task to state which view may be right, but rather to reflect on why people might believe or take part in some religious practice; to try to begin to enter into their feelings.

If there is to be time for reflection and discussion there has to be a sense of urgency about the practical activity.
For example, in the work on Easter through art (pages 42–43), or the follow-up work on the visualization of the Zacchaeus story (pages 21–24), the teacher might tell the children:

You have 10 minutes to complete your worksheet before sharing your ideas with the class.

We need to provide occasions when children can develop their imagination, intuition, creativity, and a sense of awe and wonder.
This entails opportunities for reflecting on experiences, either their own or those of real or fictional characters.

RE should be interesting and relevant, and often fun, it should grab the children's attention from the outset and promote a positive attitude. So in the examples below a variety of approaches has been used, all of which require children to play an active part.

Note

In the examples of units of work on pages 16–45, contrasting typefaces are used to distinguish the teacher's questions and responses from those of the children, as follows:

- **The teacher's questions, comments and responses are in bold type like this.**
- Children's answers, questions and comments (oral or in writing) appear in this script fount.

Life as a Journey 1

9–10 year olds

Possible Learning Outcomes

This work is designed to help children to gain experience of using language in a non-literal way, in order to appreciate the metaphorical approach to language which is characteristic of religions. The activities give children an opportunity to:

- demonstrate their understanding that life can be viewed as a journey (AT2);
- reflect on their own life journeys (AT2).

After a preliminary introduction by the teacher of the idea of life being like a journey, the children mapped their own life journeys to date. They then shared with the whole class one aspect of their life journey that was particularly important to them.

This aspect of the work could be developed by looking at the high and low points in their experience, noting that everyone has highs and lows, and considering how we can learn to cope with the low points of life.

It could also be developed by looking at the significant times in life, e.g. the rites of passage in Christianity, including baptism, confirmation, marriage and funerals.

One child drew his life journey showing how it divided into different branches, thus producing choices. This promoted much discussion as to the choices we all have and what effect they have on our lives.

The children wrote about their hopes for a happy and useful life and how they would like to be remembered:

> I would like to be remembered as a good mum and a kind and funny person to be with. I would like to be remembered for being a pathologist ... I would work for charity and give blood or maybe a kidney transplant for children. I would hate to be remembered as an unkind and ungrateful person.

> I would like to be remembered as a famous football player, a fun person and a good husband and dad. I would like to be remembered for having lots of friends and a good manager having lots of skills, scoring at least 400 goals in my career.

Follow-up discussion on this kind of written work might include:

- Why is kindness important to people?
- Is a sense of humour important? Why/why not?
- What makes a good friend?
- Does being a good friend mean we have lots of friends?
- Who or what can guide us when we make important decisions/choices?

Life as a Journey 2

This class tackled their work on life journeys in a different but equally successful way.

Possible Learning Outcomes

This work is designed to help children to:

- consider and express their own journey through life by way of introduction to the study of a religious leader's life journey (AT2).

Thought-provoking questions are essential if we are to help children reflect on their own lives and values before looking at the life journey of a great religious teacher.

Here are four questions the teacher asked, and the answers children gave. Each day for four days one question was put on the comment board, and the children were encouraged to write down their ideas. Their answers formed the basis for class discussion.

1. **What do we need to survive our journey through life?**

   love, care, help, talking, friendship, understanding, determination, faith, experience, cuddly care, thoughts, plans.

2. **What sort of map might we need to help us find our way through life?**

   a belief, advice from friends, Jesus, God, faith, looking at places, will power, advice from parents.

3. **What are the main turning-points in our journey through life?**

   going to places and meeting people, marriage, losing someone you love, having children, getting a job, buying a house.

4. **Where is our journey leading?**

   to happiness, to nothing, to heaven, to an after life, to new things and places, to live on a farm, to a good life, artist, your life stops when you die - but we don't know, to have a career, have a good job - one that I enjoy, keep out of trouble with the police, pioneer some scientific development.

Possible Written Work

If there is discussion *before* asking the children to write, then their thinking can be challenged, and they can consider the implications of what they've written on the comment board.

For questions 1 and 2 one might ask children to choose two or three words from each list and explain why they're important.

Question 3 provides an excellent opportunity to begin work on rites of passage, e.g. naming ceremonies in one or more world faith.

Question 4 could lead to work on religious and non-religious ideas about what happens after we die. One might pose another question: 'How does the way we answer question 2 and/or 4 affect the kind of life we lead?'

Younger children could reflect on their life journeys in the last twelve months – the highlights, the difficult times; the time when decisions had to be made; the signs of growth/development – and what they might look forward to in the next twelve months.

Jesus the Twelve Year Old

9–10 year olds

Possible Learning Outcomes

This work is designed to help children to:

- be able to demonstrate a knowledge and understanding of Jesus' visit to the Temple at the age of 12 (Luke 2:41–52) (AT1);
- respond to the biblical account by considering the thoughts and feelings of different characters (AT2).

The class were told how Mary and Joseph took Jesus to Jerusalem to celebrate the Passover. The children were asked to write an account of what happened from the point of view of either Jesus, or Mary and Joseph or an onlooker.

When I was twelve

One day when I was twelve I went to the Passover feast with my mum Mary and my father Joseph. When the feast was over I stayed behind while my parents started to travel home. They thought that I was with the group. When my parents got a day's journey away, they found out that I was not with them. So they came back to find me. When they found me my mother said, "son why have you treated us so badly?" "I have stayed back because I wanted to listen to the teachers and listen to their answers" I said. And my mother kept all these things in her heart.

Jesus at the Temple in Jerusalem

I ran away from dad and mum when I was twelve. I was gone for a whole day. Joseph and Mary thought I was with the group. They realized I was gone and so they set out looking for me, they found me in the temple in Jerusalem. They said "what on earth are you doing here Jesus?" so I told them! "I have to be in the house of my father." Mary said, "we looked every where for you. You worried us to death." "I was talking to the Rabbis about my father (God). I wanted advice on how to be a better person and how to be good at helping

Mary and Joseph's point of view

We had set off back to Nazareth. We thought that Jesus was with some other children. When night came Jesus could not be found. We said, "we will set off back tomorrow." We woke up in the morning and set off back to Jerusalem. When we arrived we searched high and low. After three days we found Jesus in the temple. He was talking with wise men. I said, "What are you doing here? Don't you know we have been looking for three days." "Wise men, what do you think you are doing keeping my son here?" Jesus spoke up. "Didn't you know I would be in my father's house?" I was confused but Jesus came back to Nazareth with us and was very obedient.

At the Temple in Jerusalem

I saw a young man walk into the Temple. He said his name was Jesus. He looked about 12, but he sounded about 40. The questions he asked were like "What are the stars made from?" and "how long the temple had been here?" And also he told us a lot about God, and what he wants. He never talked just about himself. He was there for about 2 days, when his parents came through, and to my surprise they said, "what are you doing, scaring us like that?" and the young boy called Jesus just answered, "Didn't you know, that I had to be in my own father's home," and then they answered "your father's home is back in Nazareth. Now come on, we have been worried to death about you, come on." I was surprised but after that, they just left from the temple, and that was the last I saw of Jesus.

Note This could be the basis of a literacy hour with a text level focus.

Jesus' Baptism and Temptations

Possible Learning Outcomes

This work is designed to help children to:

- know and be able to recount the events concerning the baptism and temptations of Jesus (AT1);
- begin to understand why the temptations were so important in the life journey of Jesus (AT1/2);
- reflect on their own temptations and the decisions they might make when tempted (AT2).

Having reflected on their own lives (see pages 16–17) these children were encouraged to look at the life of Jesus as a series of choices.

Jesus in the desert
- → **Should he use his power selfishly?**
- → **Should he obey God and help others?**
- → **Should he obey God whatever the consequences?**

The first significant event in Jesus' adult life was his baptism (Mark 1:9–13). After reading the story to the children, the teacher asked:

Why was John baptizing people?
Let's look at the clues in verses 4–5.

The children looked up the reference. The teacher then asked:

Why do you think Jesus wanted to be baptized?

Discussion with the children continued as follows:

Why do you think Jesus went into the desert after he'd been baptized by John?

He may have wanted to think about God. To clear his head.

Jesus had time to think about the future. He had to choose how to live his life; how to use the special power he'd been given.

He could choose to stay in the desert or go back to the fertile land.

He could choose to do what God said or not to do what God said.

He could choose to go back to Nazareth to carry on being a carpenter.

He could choose to do what God wanted him to do.

How would he find out what God wanted him to do? Let's find out what happened to Jesus while he was in the desert.

The story of Jesus' temptation in the desert (Matthew 4:1–11; Luke 4:1–13) was read to the children. (We used J.G. Priestley's 'The Easy Way and the Hard Way' in *Bible Stories for Classroom and Assembly: The New Testament*, RMEP.)

The children were asked to illustrate one of the temptations. Afterwards they talked about their pictures. Some portrayed the devil as a person; others as thoughts tempting Jesus.

The teacher then asked:

> **What would have happened if Jesus hadn't responded to God's call but just gone back to Nazareth?**
>
> He would have stayed as a carpenter.
> He wouldn't have healed people.
> He wouldn't have been arrested and killed.
>
> **So there wouldn't have been any Christianity. We probably wouldn't know anything about Jesus at all. What important choices he made while he was in the desert!**
>
> **When have you been tempted?**

The children sat quietly and thought about a time when they had been tempted. Then they were asked to write or draw a cartoon illustrating this occasion.

My Temptation

I was really tempted to go into my mum's bedroom and get her make-up bag off her dresser. Opening the bag I thought there is no harm in trying out a bit of this and a bit of that. By the time I had finished putting the make-up on. All of a sudden the door opened in came mum took one look at me and said where are you going? anywhere nice? can I come

Temptations

When Seamus ripped one of my favourite horse posters I was tempted to go into his room, ignoring all the pushes and shoves he gave me and shouts of 'Get out." For I would just go in and rip one of his posters. (One of his best football posters.)

People Jesus Met I: Zacchaeus

Possible Learning Outcomes

This work is designed to help children to:

- be able to recount the story of Zacchaeus (Luke 19:1–8) from different points of view (AT1);
- reflect on Zacchaeus' motivations, and the motivation that might have driven Jesus to befriend Zacchaeus (AT1/2);
- reflect on how they feel when they are excluded from a group (**younger children** – AT2);
- consider times when they are prepared to risk unpopularity (**older children** – AT2).

In order to get the children to enter into the feelings experienced in the story, 'visualization' was used.

Note The children need to have experienced 'stilling' exercises before embarking on the visualization. (See Stone, M. K. *Don't Just Do Something, Sit There*, pages 10–13, RMEP.)

The teacher began by talking about the role of Zacchaeus as a Jewish tax-collector working for the Roman occupying power, and of the attitude of other Jews towards him. The following visualization was then used:

> One of the marvellous things about using our imagination is that we can travel anywhere we like in a split second. We can also go forward or backward in time.
>
> Today, in our imagination, we're going to travel back in time to about 2000 years ago when Jesus was living in Palestine …
>
> I'd like you to sit in an alert and relaxed position …
> Close your eyes gently …
> Let your shoulders drop and feel relaxed …
> Notice your breathing … See that it's slow and regular …
>
> You live in the village of Jericho in Palestine. It's a very hot, dry place, though there are springs of water in the village. The roads are dusty tracks. Today, with all the other villagers, you are standing at the side of the road that enters the village. Everybody's talking about a man called Jesus, from Nazareth, who's coming to their village. Some people have heard him teach, tell stories, even heal people …
> You are standing there listening to what your neighbours are saying …
>
> As you stand there you feel the heat of the sun on your head and shoulders … You can smell the dryness of the dust …
>
> If you want to ask your neighbour a question about Jesus now's your chance …
>
> Suddenly, you feel someone behind you pushing in to get a view … You turn round to see who it is …
>
> It's that Jewish traitor, Zacchaeus, that little man who collects taxes for the Romans … He always collects more than he needs to and has become very rich, while the poor become even poorer…
>
> What do you do when Zacchaeus tries to push through? …
> What do you say to him? … How do you feel at this moment? …
> Realizing that he can't get through to the front, Zacchaeus goes a little further ahead. While you're waiting for Jesus to come you watch Zacchaeus and see him climb a tree further along the road and climb out along a branch stretching right out over the road … Nobody else seems to have seen him.
>
> Suddenly, you hear the crowds cheering. Jesus must be coming … You strain forward to see him … You can see him … How do you feel at this particular moment? …
>
> As Jesus walks by you he looks up into the tree where Zacchaeus is hiding. Notice the expression on Jesus's face …
>
> You're surprised that Jesus has seen Zacchaeus hidden by the leaves and with so many other people around him. He looks as if he's about to speak to Zacchaeus. You must warn him what kind of man Zacchaeus is. What do you say to Jesus as you call out the warning? …
>
> Jesus appears to ignore what you say, for you hear him speak to Zacchaeus: 'Come down out of the tree, Zacchaeus. I'd like to come home and have a meal with you.'
>
> Notice the expression on Zacchaeus' face as Jesus speaks to him …

Everyone else gasps in amazement. Then they start muttering and grumbling. Listen to the kind of things they're saying … This seems a very different crowd from the one that was cheering Jesus only a few moments ago.

As people start moving away you stand and wonder why Jesus spoke to Zacchaeus at all … and why he's going to his home … You decide to follow … Keep your distance …

You stand by an open window in Zacchaeus's home and can hear every word that's said. You hear this horrible little tax-collector welcoming Jesus, and you can smell appetizing smells which make you realize how hungry you are; but you're so curious you decide to wait and continue listening.

You hear Zacchaeus say, 'You know, I've treated people very unfairly. I'm going to count up all I have and I shall give half of it to the poor, and those I've cheated I'll give four times as much back to them.' You wonder what has made Zacchaeus such a changed person …

As you leave and walk home you have so much to think about … Why did Jesus talk to Zacchaeus in the first place? Didn't he realize that this would turn people against him? … Was it sensible to behave like this? … What advice would you like to give Jesus? … Or what questions would you like to ask him?

And now you're going to leave Jericho and return to the classroom ….

Wriggle your toes … Feel the hardness of the chair under you … Take a long slow breath, and when you're ready open your eyes and have a good stretch.

After visualizing the story the teacher asked three questions:

How did members of the crowd feel about Zacchaeus?

How do you think Zacchaeus felt about himself?

When Jesus had dinner with Zacchaeus what do you think Jesus said to him?

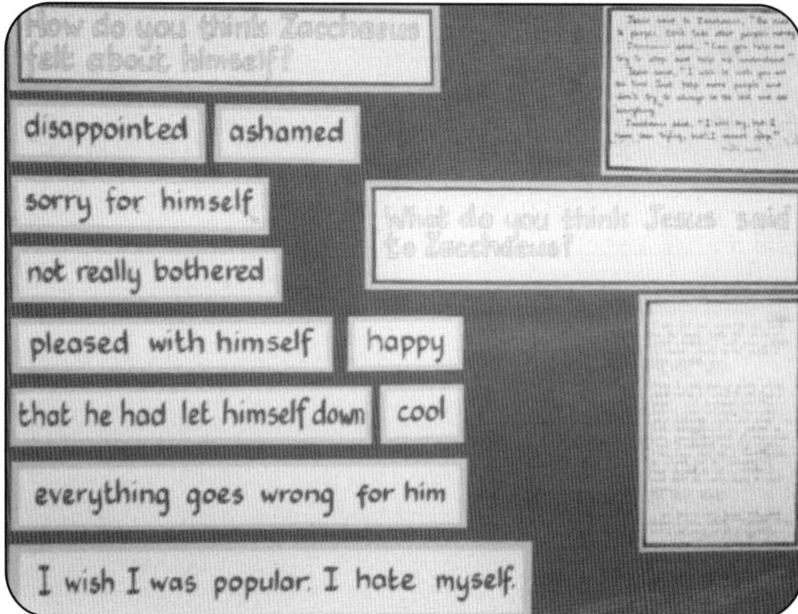

The children's answers were written on the board so that they could be discussed more fully, especially where apparent contradictions occurred.

There was discussion about how and why Zacchaeus had changed. The children were asked to illustrate this change either by writing a two-verse poem, or by using colour and form to express Zacchaeus' feelings before and after he met Jesus or by writing some prose.

Come on. Let's go
To a house to collect
Kick, bang, knock on the door.
'Search in your pocket!
Give us some more!

Here you go, lady,
Have some coins.
One ... two .... three .... four.... five ...
Oh, and some for your child.
I don't know, I'm going wild!

'Why do you tax
people, Zacchaeus?'
'Because I enjoy it and it's fun.'
'Yes, but if people were taxing you, and
taking all your money, would it be fun then, eh?'
'No ... but people aren't taxing me, Jesus.'
'No, but they might.
Greed has spoiled you.'
'You're right. I'll change my ways.'

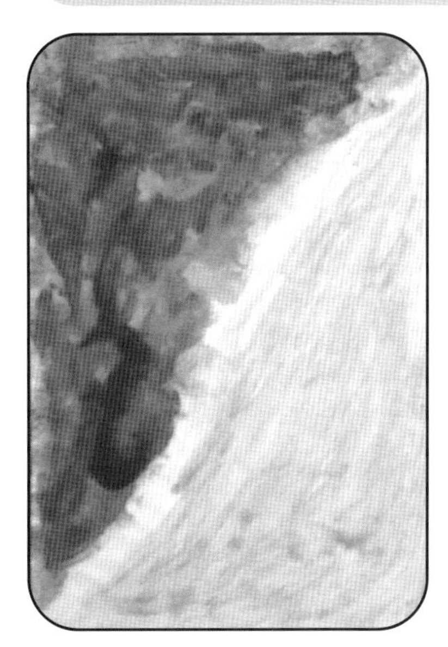

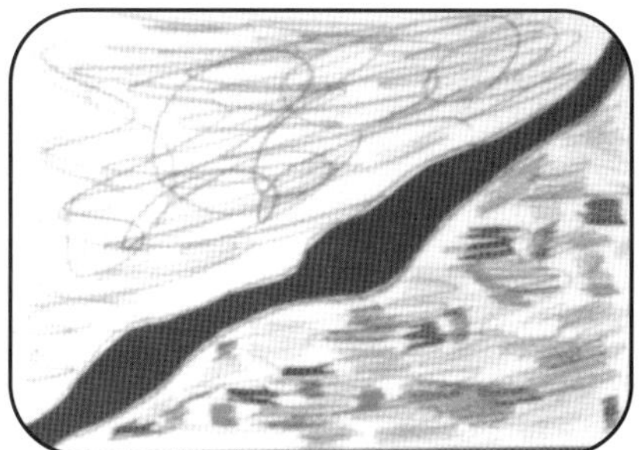

At the end of the lesson the children shared their work with the whole class.

This work could be followed up in various ways so that what the children have learnt is related to their own experience.

If the focus of attention is on Zacchaeus the teacher might ask:

How do you feel if you're left out?
(Younger children could draw a picture or write their feelings, i.e. thought bubbles.)

How do you feel if you're ignored?

How do you feel if no one will play with you?

Is there anything we can do to make sure that no one is left out?

The teacher could encourage the children to try putting their ideas into practice and to report back in the following lesson.

For **older children** the focus of attention may well be on Jesus and the way in which he behaved: risking his popularity by befriending an outcast; making himself vulnerable. Then the teacher might ask:

Are there times when we're willing to lose our popularity in order to help/support someone who isn't popular/liked?

Attribute Cubes

Another way of reflecting on the change that took place in the life of Zacchaeus is to make use of attribute cubes, but before the children are asked to make one for Zacchaeus they should make a personal cube for themselves (see diagram overleaf).

The cubes should be made out of card and sufficiently large for the children to write clearly.

Making a personal cube is a very popular activity causing a great deal of interest and fun. There is seldom time for every child to share the details of their cube with the whole class, but sharing with their neighbours ensures that everyone participates.

Class discussion may focus on squares 3, 4 and 5 and provide the teacher with an opportunity to value the differences as well as the similarities. It's important that children know that they don't have to be the same as their peers.

Having reflected on their own attributes it is now time to make a Zacchaeus cube.

The changes that took place will become most evident if squares 3–6 are divided into triangles, with the left /top triangles used for Zacchaeus' attitudes *before* he met Jesus, and the right/lower triangles for those *after* he met Jesus.

The variety of answers the children produce provide different insights into the changing character of Zacchaeus. During class discussion that follows paired-sharing the children should be encouraged to elaborate. The discussion can also be an opportunity for children to ask each other questions about the character of Zacchaeus.

With **younger children** one large, class cube could be made with a variety of answers written on each face. These could then be used as a focus for discussion:

Could all these answers be right? Why/Why not?

Which do you think are the best ideas? Why?

Child's name
1.

Where do you come from?
2.

What's important in your life?
3.

What's important to everybody?
4.

What do you enjoy?
5.

A characteristic of yourself?
6.

Personal

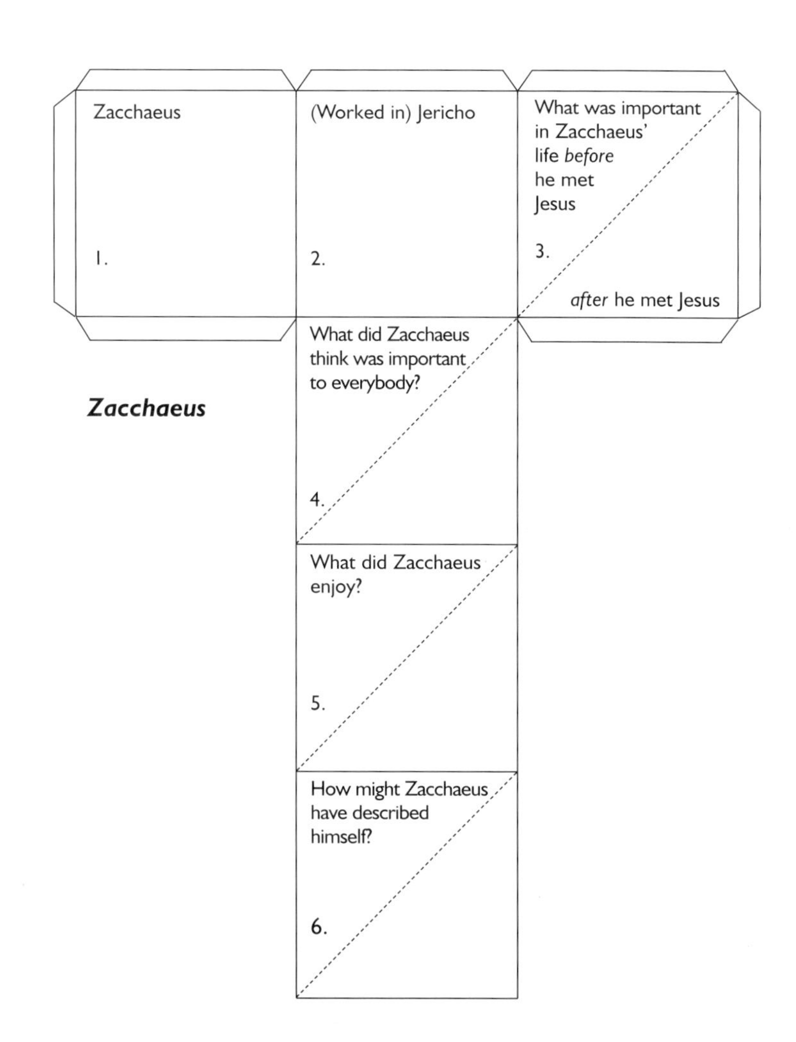

People Jesus Met 2: The Roman Centurion

Possible Learning Outcomes

This work is designed to help children to:

- be able to recount the story of the Roman centurion and suggest reasons for his behaviour (AT1/2);
- enter imaginatively into other people's experiences (AT2);
- be able to reflect on what motives drive them (AT2).

When Jesus entered Capernaum, a Roman officer met him and begged him for help: "Sir, my servant is sick in bed at home, unable to move and suffering terribly".

"I will go and make him well," Jesus said.

"Oh no, sir," answered the officer. "I do not deserve to have you come into my house. Just give the order, and my servant will get well. I, too, am a man under the authority of superior officers, and I have soldiers under me. I order this one, 'Go!' and he goes; and I order that one, 'Come!' and he comes; and I order my slave, 'Do this!' and he does it".

When Jesus heard this, he was surprised and said to the people following him, "I tell you, I have never found anyone in Israel with faith like this. I assure you that many will come from the east and the west and sit down with Abraham, Isaac and Jacob at the feast in the Kingdom of heaven. But those who should be in the Kingdom will be thrown out into the darkness, where they will cry and grind their teeth."

Then Jesus said to the officer, "Go home, and what you believe will be done for you."

And the officer's servant was healed that very moment.

Matthew 8:5–13 (*Good News Bible*)

This account of another encounter with Jesus by a person most Jews would have hated was also explored using visualization. The following notes explain how to use the visualization provided on pages 26–27.

Preparation

1. Children should have experienced 'stilling' exercises before embarking on visualization. This eliminates potential problems concerned with difficulties children may experience in sitting still. (See, for example, Stone, M. K. *Don't Just Do Something, Sit There*, RMEP.)
2. Be clear what you want to get out of this story.
3. Feel free to alter the text – to extend, shorten or change the words.
4. But remember always:

- to speak in the present tense. (It's happening *now*.)
- to include as many of the senses as possible. (This will help it come alive.)
- to ensure there are sufficient pauses to allow children to respond to the situation they find themselves in. (The dots indicate such pauses.)
- to keep the statements and questions as open-ended as possible, giving children the opportunity to make it *their* story.

5. Decide which parts of the visualization you wish to discuss in detail. (Asterisks by the text could indicate these.)

Introduction

1. Start with children's own experience. Discuss how appearances can be deceptive; how easy it is to misjudge people; seeing people as stereotypes and not as individual human beings. Give an example, e.g. someone who looks slight of stature but in fact shows tremendous stamina as a long-distance runner, or recall situations that have happened to you, e.g. children saying they hate Germans after seeing them as the enemy, 'the baddies' in war films, and then meeting one and being surprised at how friendly this German is.
2. Children can be told or read the story (from the *Good News Bible*) and need to understand something of the background, i.e.

- that Judaea was under Roman occupation;
- how the Romans may have felt towards the Jews;

- that there was a local garrison of 100 soldiers under a centurion;
- that most centurions would have shown little interest in the 'natives' but this centurion was different, and was prepared to show respect – and in a public place too!
- that this centurion recognized the power and authority of Jesus;
- how Jewish people may have felt towards the Roman occupying power, e.g. how they would have felt when forced to carry a Roman soldier's baggage (see Matthew 6:41–42).

The Visualization

One of the marvellous things about using our imagination is that we can travel anywhere we like in a split second. We can also go forward and backward in time.

Today, in our imagination, we're going to travel back in time nearly 2000 years to when Jesus was living in the country called Judaea …

I'd like you to sit in an alert and relaxed position …
Close your eyes gently …
Let your shoulders drop … Feel relaxed …
Now concentrate on your breathing …
Breathe slowly, deeply and very quietly …
As you breathe in feel the breath travelling to all parts of your body giving you life and strength.

You live in the land of Judaea, the land in which Jesus was born and grew up … It is a land governed not by your people, the Jews, but by the Romans, who show little interest or respect for the Jewish people. They even have a garrison in your town, so you're constantly reminded that you're not a free people. When you see a Roman soldier how do you feel? …

Up in the north of the country is the town of Capernaum, on the western shore of the Sea of Galilee, on the great trade route from Damascus to Acco and Tyre. This is where you live. You see many strangers from far countries, selling their goods in the market place. You can actually smell the dust ….

Feel the warmth of the sun on your head and shoulders ….

As you stand at the side of the road you see people in long flowing clothes, many with their heads covered, walking past, talking with their friends and neighbours. Suddenly you hear a different kind of sound; a buzz of excitement; everybody seeming to talk at the same time … Everyone gathers together looking expectantly down the road … You join the crowd … Ask someone what's happening … Is someone important coming? … Could it be the man Jesus you've heard so much about but never seen? That would be something to tell your family when you get home. You remember what you've heard of this man, Jesus … that he has unusual power, and that he uses his power to heal people. You wonder why he doesn't use his power to lead a Jewish army and drive the Romans out of the country. All your people would be free again. No more Roman taxes.

Hold on a minute. While you've been daydreaming you've nearly missed something important. Jesus is coming. Can you see him? Are some of his friends, his disciples with him? But wait … someone else is coming from the opposite direction. Make way for him …You recognize this soldier, this centurion, in charge of the garrison. You move right back. You don't want to be in trouble with this man of all men! He seems to be heading straight towards Jesus. What do you think is going to happen? ... Is the centurion going to arrest Jesus? … Or walk by and ignore him?

No, he's stopped in front of Jesus and is speaking to him. Everyone stops talking or moving. You all lean forward to try and hear what is being said. Here is this tall, proud centurion speaking to Jesus in all earnestness. 'Sir, will you help me?' Fancy a Roman addressing a Jew with respect! And then asking for his help … You look at your neighbour and you both look amazed …

Would Jesus help an enemy? You wonder … Your neighbour says to you, 'Surely we all want to kill the enemy not help him.' What would you have said if the centurion had asked you for help? You listen to how Jesus replies: 'In what way can I help you?' 'It's not me who needs the help, it's my servant. He's very ill, he can't move and is in great pain.' 'Don't worry,' says Jesus, 'I'll come straight away and make him well.'

The people around you start muttering about Jesus … What are they saying? … What do you say to them? …

When you see the centurion about to speak again you all stop muttering.

'It's all right,' says the centurion. 'You don't need to come all the way to my house. Just say the word and I know my servant will be healed. I've been watching you recently and I know you're something special. I know you have power. I recognize power when I see it. I have some power myself. If I give an order to one of my soldiers or a servant, "Go and get..." he goes. If I say, "Come," he comes. You only have to say that my servant is healed and I know he will be.' You listen intently ... Jesus turns and faces the crowd. He seems to be looking straight at you ... What kind of expression has he on his face? Does he look angry, ... scared ... or what? ... Jesus is speaking: 'I haven't heard anything like this from my own people. He's a better man than most of us. God doesn't think it important what race we belong to. He sees everyone as an individual human being. We all know there are good and bad Jews. There are good Romans as well as bad Romans too.'

While you're thinking about what Jesus has said you see him turn round to face the Roman again and say to him, 'You can go home, and when you get home you'll find your servant well again. Your faith has made your servant well.' Look at the Roman centurion's face as he turns and strides off home to find his servant is indeed well again.

People crowd round Jesus. They can hardly believe their eyes and their ears. Is Jesus really going to help heal the enemy? All around you people are arguing amongst themselves as to what kind of leader Jesus is ... You join in. What do you say?

As you walk slowly home are you happy or disappointed? ... You think about what you've just heard and seen, and what you'll tell your family ...

What questions do you think your family will ask you when you've told them what you've seen and heard? ...

And now we're going to leave Capernaum and return to the classroom ...

Wriggle your toes and feel the hardness of your chairs ...

And when you're ready open your eyes and have a good stretch ...

Debriefing

1. Children need the opportunity to share their imaginary experiences. They could do this in pairs before having a general class discussion. You might ask them what surprised them most; which part they enjoyed or didn't enjoy; which part they found the most difficult to visualize.
2. Ask the children if they have any questions about the visualization. Encourage other children to help you answer them.

Possible Activities

Think of activities that provide opportunities for children to express their experience. (If possible give children a choice.) Here are some suggestions, but don't give children all these options or they may spend all the available time deciding!

- Write down what you tell your family about this first time you see Jesus. Don't forget the arguments you heard in the crowd, and your own feelings. You might like to end by telling your family whether you think Jesus is the kind of man you'd want to follow.
- Role-play the whole event (suitable for **any age group**).
- Role-play two Jews who have opposing views about Jesus (suitable for **older children**).
- Write down what you think Jesus should have done. Was he right to help the centurion? Give your reasons.
- Be a journalist and interview Jesus or the centurion.
- Make a poster headed 'Surprising Event'.

There should always be time to share and discuss!

Possible Follow-Up Work

Children could consider what influences them when making judgements of other people, e.g.

- membership of a group,
- what people wear,
- physical attributes,
- the opinions of others.

Ask if children have learnt anything from the biblical account that challenges them and their behaviour towards others.

The Teaching of Jesus 1: Gospel Quotations

10–11 year olds

Possible Learning Outcomes

This work on the teaching of Jesus (pages 28–29) is designed to help children to:

- know some of the teaching of Jesus (AT1);
- be able to explain what they think the teaching means (AT1/2);
- reflect on important values in their own lives and share their thinking with others (AT2).

Before leaving primary school many children have learned something about the Bible. They know stories from it, but generally very little work is done about the teaching it contains.

These children used the gospel quotations on the right as an opportunity to examine some of the teaching of Jesus. The quotations were enlarged and the class worked in pairs, to ensure that the more reticent children took part. Each pair was given one quotation and was asked:

What do you think this quotation means?

Are there any questions you would like to ask about it?

What do you think would happen if all Christians followed this teaching?

This was followed by a time of sharing. Some children thought the teaching was highly impracticable. Others thought it an ideal worth striving for.

The teacher wrote on the board:

If someone asked you, 'What are the three main principles that guide your life?' what would you say?

After a short discussion on the meaning of 'principles', the children wrote down their answers, which they then shared with their neighbours. This was followed by class discussion during which the children were challenged to justify their ideas.

Gospel Quotations Used

You have heard that people were told in the past, 'An eye for an eye, and a tooth for a tooth.' But I tell you: do not take revenge on someone who wrongs you.

(Matthew 5:38–39)

You have heard that it was said, 'Love your friends, hate your enemies.' But now I tell you, love your enemies and pray for those who persecute you.

(Matthew 5:43)

If you forgive others the wrongs they have done to you, your Father in heaven will also forgive you.

(Matthew 6:14)

Treat other people as you would like them to treat you.

(Luke 6:31)

Love the Lord your God with all your heart and soul and with all your strength, and with all your mind. Love your neighbour as yourself.

(Luke 10:27)

Why should God reward you if you only love people who love you? That's what everyone else does!

(Luke 6:32)

The Teaching of Jesus 2: 'I am the vine, you are the branches.' (John 15:5)

The teacher asked:

What is a vine?

How important are the roots?

What are the branches for?

How can you be sure of a good harvest?

What's the role of the gardener?

Following the discussion the teacher read the first five verses of John 15 (from the *Good News Bible*), then said, 'Perhaps the words "A branch cannot bear fruit by itself; it can only do so if it remains in the vine," mean that just as branches have to be attached to and nourished by the vine, so Christians have to be "attached" to Jesus or follow his way of living. If they are to follow Jesus' way of living they must know what he was like.'

The teacher then asked:

What was Jesus like?

Kind, helpful, trustworthy, able to tell right from wrong, true to his word, sharing and caring, set a good example, honest, not selfish.

The teacher encouraged the children to give examples where possible then asked:

What are the 'roots' that have helped us to grow?

Food, parents, friends and family, love and care, knowledge, thinking, religion, beliefs, praying, faith in yourself, faith in God, courage from inside yourself.

Sit quietly and think what has been the most important root in helping you to grow. When you've thought, write it on a strip of paper that looks like a root, and we'll stick it on our Tree of Life.

(The first two children to finish painted a large tree and the whole class saw their roots attached.)

Each child read their root and then the class was asked:

Have we left anything out?

Well-nourished roots produce good fruit. What fruit would you hope to produce? When you've thought, write it on a piece of fruit and we'll stick them all on our tree.

Once again all the ideas were shared. The lesson ended with a careful look at the relationship between the words on the roots and those on the fruit.

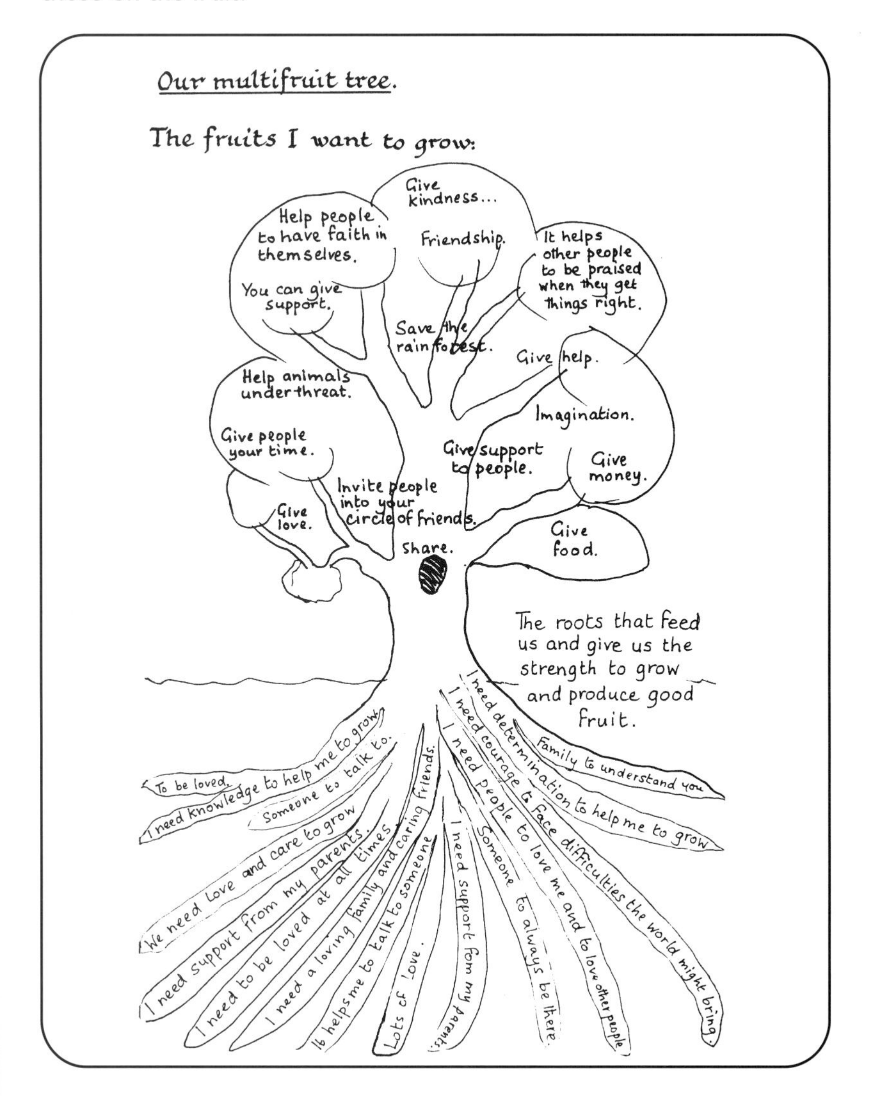

This work is appropriate for **any age group**.

The Teaching of Jesus 2: 'I am the vine, you are the branches.' (John 15:5)

9–10 year olds

Overturning the Temple Tables

7–9 year olds

Possible Learning Outcomes

This work is designed to help children to:

- know that Jesus became angry when he saw stalls set up in the Court of the Gentiles (AT1);
- reflect on what made him angry and behave in the way he did (AT1/2);
- reflect on their own anger, and how 'righteous anger' can have positive effects (AT2).

First, this class shared ideas as to what made them angry. These were listed on the board. Then they were asked:

Are they all the same kind of anger?

Most of the examples concerned themselves being hurt in some way. One or two spoke of hurt to pets making them angry, and the teacher said this could be described as righteous anger; having a right to be angry on someone else's behalf.

On the board, the teacher drew a simple diagram of the Temple showing the Court of the Gentiles as the outermost court, open to all, but the only one where Gentiles, non-Jews, were allowed to pray. She explained how people came to sacrifice; how they had to use Temple money, hence the money-changers; how they would then purchase a bird or animal without blemish as a sacrifice, and how all this buying and selling took place in the Court of the Gentiles.

The account of Jesus overturning the tables in the Temple (Matthew 21:12–13) was explored using the following visualization. (For more information on using visualization, see Stone, M.K. *Don't Just Do Something, Sit There,* pages 10–13, RMEP.)

The Visualization

You're in the very busy city of Jerusalem. The streets are full of people. As you walk along with your friend, you notice a crowd of people all going in the same direction. 'Who are they following?' you wonder. 'They're following Jesus!' your friend exclaims. 'You know; that man I was telling you about; the one who heals people and tells the most wonderful stories? Let's follow him!' … As you join the crowd you wonder where Jesus is going … The Temple! ... You see Jesus walking up the steps into the Temple. You race up the steps after him so that you and your friend are at the front of the crowd … Jesus enters the outer courtyard, the only courtyard that people who aren't Jews are allowed to enter … It's the one place where these people called Gentiles might worship God … but it's not quiet at all! … You see Jesus stop and look around … You look around too … You see lots of people changing their money for the special Temple money which is used for offerings … There are traders selling all sorts of things: animals and birds for sacrifice … The courtyard is so crowded … As you stand, there listen to the sounds … sounds of people shouting, bargaining … What smells are you aware of?

Jesus moves purposefully to the nearest stall, and to your surprise he takes hold of it, lifts the edge and overturns it! Crash! There is a sudden silence … Everyone turns to see what is happening … You continue to watch … Money is rolling all over the courtyard … The stallholder is on his hands and knees trying to pick up as many coins as he can find …

To everyone's horror or surprise Jesus doesn't stop there. He overturns the next stall …. and the next … . Seeing what's happening the other stallholders quickly collect their money and goods and hurry out … Then you hear Jesus's voice above the noise of everyone talking and shouting … 'Don't the Scriptures say: "God's house shall be a place of prayer?" But you have made it into a den of robbers!'

As you leave the Temple you see the chief priest and some of his officers come to see what all the trouble is about … They look very angry too … You overhear one of them say: 'We'd better get rid of this trouble-maker, but not with this crowd all around him.' …

As you walk home you know your family will be very excited to hear that you've seen Jesus, this great teacher and healer … How will you explain his strange behaviour? …

Immediately after the visualization the teacher said: 'Tell your partner what you think of Jesus's behaviour.'

This was followed by a general sharing of reactions, and answering the questions:

Why was Jesus so angry?

Was it because someone hurt him?

Did he hurt anyone?

The children were then asked to think of one occasion when they were angry but nothing good came out of it, and one occasion when their anger led them to help someone else.

They were asked to portray their ideas on shields.

The lesson ended with the children realizing that anger can provoke people into doing something positive to improve life for other people.

Possible Follow-Up Work

If one wanted to show righteous anger in another religion, the Islamic story about Muhammad and the camel would fit in well. In this story, Muhammad rebukes a camel-driver for not looking after the needs of his camel before attending to his personal needs.

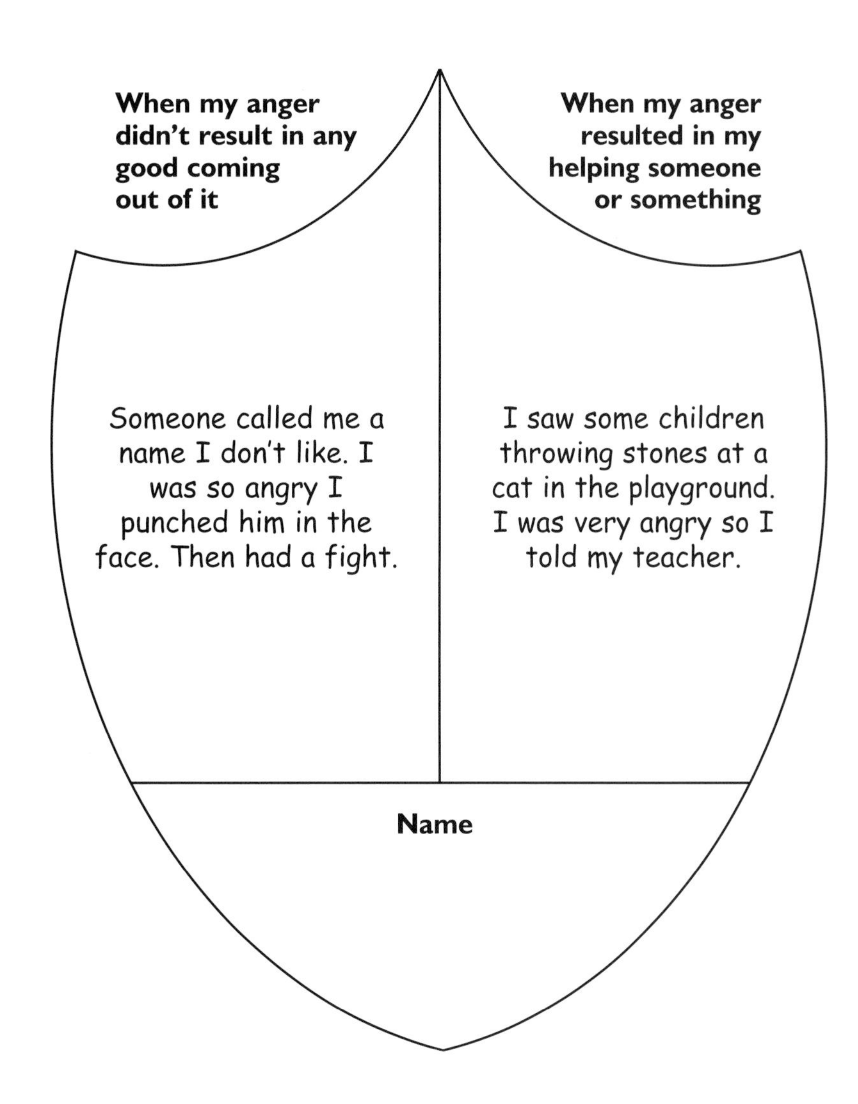

In the Garden of Gethsemane I

9–10 year olds

Possible Learning Outcomes

This work is designed to help children to:

- be able to recount what happened in the Garden of Gethsemane (AT1);
- reflect on the feelings of the disciples during and after Jesus' arrest (AT1 and AT2);
- recall times when they have let people down, and whether it was possible to make amends (AT2).

The lesson began with a discussion around three questions:

***When* have you felt let down?**

When my sheepdog wouldn't do what it was trained to do.

A friend promised to give a message to my mum saying I'd be late home, and he didn't.

I felt I'd let everyone down when I missed the penalty.

How do you *feel* if you've been let down?

Annoyed, hurt deep inside, disgraced, sad, can't trust them, dismayed, angry, disappointed, depressed, livid.

***Who* should you be able to trust?**

Parents, best friend, God, Jesus, teacher, dog, brothers and sisters.

The teacher then read the account of the disciples letting Jesus down in the Garden of Gethsemane. (J.G. Priestley tells the story well in *Bible Stories for Classroom and Assembly: The New Testament*, RMEP.)

Four headings related to the story were listed on the board:

Peter's indignation: 'I'll die first!'
'Are you asleep?' Peter's reaction.
Jesus praying.
Peter watching Jesus being arrested.

The children split up into groups of three and were asked to 'freeze' a position which demonstrated the thoughts and feelings experienced. After several minutes practising each group 'froze' and the remainder of the class were asked to guess what the actors may have been thinking at that time.

Peter denying that he'll let Jesus down ►

'I can't betray you.'
'I'll be your friend for ever.'
'I won't betray you!'
'I'm so astonished at what you're saying.'

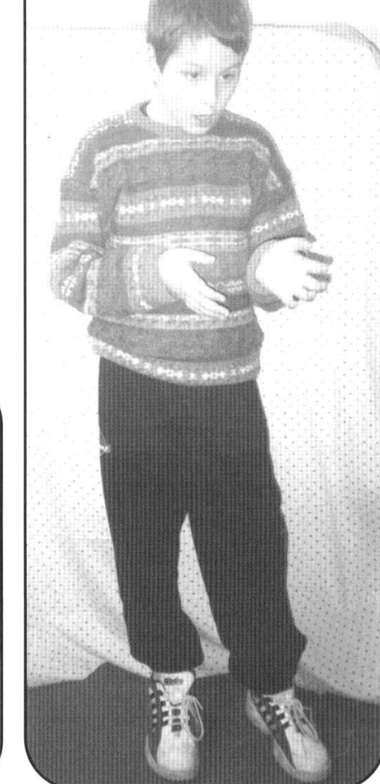

▲

When Jesus wakes the disciples they are:

Surprised, shocked, scared, ashamed, upset, heart-broken.

Jesus prays: What might he have been saying to God? ►

I need your help.
I don't want to die.
What should I do?
Please help me!
I'm scared.

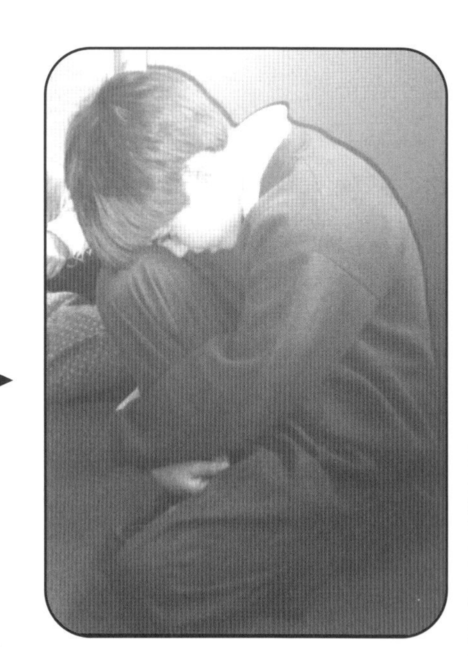

The hiding disciples watch as Jesus is led away ►

They feel ashamed of themselves.

They feel scared, frightened.

'What have I done to let Jesus be arrested?'

'Why did Jesus allow himself to be arrested?'

This work could be used with **younger or older children**.

Possible Follow-up Work

Consider:

Have you ever let anyone down?
Why was this?
How did you feel?
Were you able to make amends in any way?

Has anyone ever let you down?
Why was this, do you think?
How did you feel?
What was the result?

In the Garden of Gethsemane 2

9–10 year olds

Possible Learning Outcomes

This work is designed to help children to:

- be able to recount what happened in the Garden of Gethsemane (AT1);
- reflect on the feelings of the disciples during and after Jesus' arrest (AT1 and AT2);
- recall times when they have let people down, and whether it was possible to make amends (AT2).

Having told the story of Jesus praying in the Garden of Gethsemane and his arrest (Mark 14:43–52), the teacher asked the children to imagine the possible feelings, first of Jesus, then of the disciples, particularly Peter.

The children were then asked to think about either Jesus or Peter and to select coloured pastels that would represent their feelings. Using the pastels on sugar paper the children produced non-representational pictures. They were invited to write three key words expressing their feelings in a corner of their picture, and then to write a paragraph describing those feelings more fully.

The quiet time of selecting and using the coloured pastels gave the children time to think quite deeply.

Jesus' feelings

The soldiers led me away. I felt worried and sad. I felt worried because I might die, and I felt sad because all my friends had left me.

LES

Jesus' feelings

The soldiers led me away. All I could see was pitch black. One of the soldiers was prodding his fingers in my back and whispering behind me. I felt so embarrassed and let down. My own believers disappointed me. Disappointed, embarrassed and abused I was taken away, with my hands tied and the blindfold still covering my eyes.

HAYLEY

Resurrection

Possible Learning Outcomes

This work is designed to help children to:

- study the Resurrection accounts in three gospels and to demonstrate their comprehension of the text (AT1 – this also has potential as a literacy activity);
- reflect on the meaning of the Resurrection for Christians (AT1/2);
- reflect on their own personal beliefs (AT2).

In many schools the Easter story ends with the Crucifixion, with scant reference to the Resurrection. To begin to understand Christianity children need to know and reflect on the centrality of the Resurrection in Christian belief and practice.

First the teacher recapped what the children already knew and understood about Good Friday:

What happened on Good Friday?

Why do Christians call it 'Good Friday'?

How do you think the disciples felt on Easter Saturday?

Really upset, mad that he's dead, angry at the Jewish leaders, angry at the Romans, sorry for themselves, afraid that they might be arrested.

How do we know about these stories concerning Jesus' death?

The teacher introduced the unexpected happenings of Easter Sunday by asking the children to work in pairs as if they were detectives looking for clues and asking questions.

Each pair was given a gospel account of the Resurrection and a list of questions (see right and overleaf). They were asked to read through the passage before attempting to answer the questions. The passages used were Matthew 28:1–10, Mark 16:1–8, Luke 24:1–11.

Questions for Each Gospel Account

1. **Who visited the tomb?**
2. **When?**
3. **Write down the words that express their feelings.**
4. **Who gave them a message?**
5. **What important things did the message contain?**
6. **What questions do you want to ask?**
7. **What is the most surprising part of the account?**

Resurrection (Matthew 28 1-10.)

1. After the Sabbath, as Sunday morning was dawning, Mary Magdalene and the other Mary went to look at the tomb.
2. Suddenly there was a violent earthquake: an angel of the Lord came down from heaven, rolled the stone away and sat on it.
3. His appearance was like lightning, and his clothes were white as snow.
4. The guards were so afraid that they trembled and became like dead men.
5. The angel spoke to the women. "You must not be afraid," he said. "I know you are looking for Jesus, who was crucified.
6. He is not here; he has been raised, just as he said. Come here and see the place where he was lying.
7. Go quickly now, and tell his disciples, 'He has been raised from death and now he is going to Galilee ahead of you; there you will see him!' Remember what I have told you."
8. So they left the tomb in a hurry, afraid and yet filled with joy, and ran to tell his disciples.
9. Suddenly Jesus met them and said, "Peace be with you." They came up to him, took hold of his feet, and worshipped him.
10. Do not be afraid," Jesus said to them. "Go and tell my brothers to go to Galilee, and there they will see me."

(Good News Bible)

Resurrection.

(Mark 16 1-8.)

1. After the Sabbath was over, Mary Magdalene, Mary the mother of James, and Salome brought spices to go and anoint the body of Jesus.
2. Very early on Sunday morning, at sunrise, they went to the tomb.

3-4. On the way they said to one another, "Who will roll away the stone for us from the entrance to the tomb?" (It was a very large stone.) They looked up and saw that the stone had already been rolled back.

5. So they entered the tomb, where they saw a young man sitting on the right, wearing a white robe ~ and they were alarmed.
6. "Don't be alarmed," he said. "I know you are looking for Jesus of Nazareth, who was crucified. He is not here ~ he has been raised! Look, here is the place where they put him. Now go and give this message to his disciples, including Peter: 'He is going to Galilee ahead of you; there you will see him, just as he told you.'"
8. So they went out and ran from the tomb, distressed and terrified. They said nothing to anyone, because they were afraid.

(Good News Bible)

Resurrection.

(Luke 24 1-11.)

1. Very early on Sunday morning the women went to the tomb, carrying the spices they had prepared.
2. They found the stone rolled away from the entrance to the tomb,
3. so they went in; but they did not find the body of the Lord Jesus.
4. They stood there puzzled about this, when suddenly two men in bright shining clothes stood by them.
5. Full of fear, the women bowed down to the ground, as the men said to them, "Why are you looking among the dead for one who is alive?
6. He is not here; he has been raised. Remember what he said to you while he was in Galilee:
7. 'The Son of Man must be handed over to sinners, be crucified, and three days later rise to life.'"
8. Then the women remembered his words,
9. returned from the tomb, and told all these things to the eleven disciples and all the rest.
10. The women were Mary Magdalene, Joanna and Mary the mother of James; they and the other women with them told these things to the apostles.
11. But the apostles thought that what the women said was nonsense, and they did not believe them.
12. But Peter got up and ran to the tomb; he bent down and saw the linen wrappings but nothing else. Then he went back home amazed at what had happened.

(Good News Bible)

Resurrection accounts				
	Matthew (28:1–10)	**Mark (16:1–8)**	**Luke (24:1–11)**	**Similarities**
Who visited the tomb?	Mary Magdalene and the other Mary	Mary Magdalene, Mary mother of James, Salome	The women, Mary Magdalene, Joanna and Mary mother of James	
When?	As Sunday morning was dawning	Very early on Sunday morning	Very early on Sunday morning	
Write the words that express their feelings	Guards – trembled and were afraid Women – afraid and then filled with joy	Alarmed Distressed Terrified Afraid	Puzzled Full of fear Disciples thought it nonsense Peter – amazed	
Who gave them a message?	An angel Jesus – Go to Galilee	A young man	Two men in bright shining clothes	
What important things did the message contain?	Don't be afraid. Jesus has been raised. You'll see him in Galilee.	Don't be afraid. Jesus has been raised. You'll see him in Galilee.	He is not here, he has been raised.	

When the children had completed most, if not all of the questions the teacher went through the first five and wrote the answers on a grid on the board, as above.

Then the children looked for similarities and built up a picture of what they thought could have happened.

The questions they asked included:

> Why did Jesus go to Galilee?
>
> Who were the two men in Luke?
>
> How was the stone rolled away?
>
> Is Jesus still in Galilee now?
>
> Where is he now?
>
> Is it a true story?

(The last three questions clearly show the need to include some work about the Ascension and Pentecost. See, for example, the companion book Ewens, A. and Stone, M.K. *Teaching about God, Worship and Spirituality*, RMEP.)

The children were invited to help in the answering of the questions whilst retaining a sense of mystery.

RESURRECTION

Easter Saturday

I'm afraid of the Romans, terrified they might find me, but God might help me.

Easter Sunday

Speechless with joy, relieved with happiness, glad to talk with him again

By Isaac

RESURRECTION

Easter Saturday

Endlessly thinking of things that I have forgotten to say to Jesus.
Angry at the way people acted towards him.
Sleepless I lie in my bed thinking of him.
Troubled at the way people treated him.
Enemies are coming into my life every day.
Restless, I want to get things over and done with.

Easter Sunday

Excited, I welcome him back.
Amazed, I ask how he came back.
Speechless, I sit beside him.
Tremendously, he tells me his story.
Extraordinary things had happened, he told me.
Relieved, we sit down in friendship.

Written Work

The children wrote poems, making use of the words on the board but not limited by them. Verse 1 was to reflect the feelings on Easter Saturday, and verse 2 those on Easter Sunday.

Concluding Discussion

What do you think Christians will learn from this story?
Do they believe that people who have died come back to life?

There is still hope.

When people know that Jesus came back to life it could help them do something that they weren't confident about. Also if someone close died, it would help them to get over it.

What do you believe?

(The emphasis here should be on accepting and respecting diversity of belief.)

Easter: Reflecting on Memorials

Possible Learning Outcomes

This work is designed to help children to:

- develop their knowledge and understanding of Christianity by encountering some of the important beliefs about Jesus, and how Christians remember Jesus today (AT1);
- enhance their own spiritual development through sharing ways in which they remember people and pets who are no longer alive (AT2);
- consider how they would like to be remembered (AT2).

Memorials provided a way in for this class to consider how Christians remember Jesus. (This approach is well illustrated in the video *Eggshells and Thunderbolts*, BBC Education.)

Lesson 1

The starting-point was:

> **How do you remember people or pets who are no longer alive?**

The children brought in objects that helped them recall people, pets and incidents concerning them, such as a walking-stick, photographs, a locket, the collar of a pet dog, a book. They talked about their object and their memories and were then asked to write about them.

The written work isn't the end, for these kinds of passages raise questions about how we cope with the loss of loved ones and that sadness is a natural reaction. The fish dying might also raise the issue of responsibility: What have we learnt from this death? How will it affect our future treatment of pets?

My Auntie Margaret

I was sad when my Auntie Margaret died in 1991 of leukaemia. She was 54 when she died. My mum, dad, nana, gramps, Uncle Stan and all the children were so upset about it that my nana never ate anything for about 2 or 3 days. She was heart-broken.

The Day My Fish Died

One morning, when I was eight, I got up to feed my fish and it was floating on the top of the tank. It must have died in the night because I never fed it for a day and I never cleaned it out for two days. I buried it in my bit of garden. When I dig my bit of the garden I always think of him.

Lesson 2

Here the children considered and then wrote about how they would like to be remembered:

In Memoriam

When I die I would like to be remembered for being friendly and for being a good friend. I would like to be remembered for this because I try hard to be friendly even if I don't really like the person.

I would also like to be remembered for being enthusiastic and good at sport because I enjoy it and normally try my hardest.

When I grow up I would like to be a father so I hope I'll get remembered for being a good dad because I like young children and babies.

I would quite like to be remembered for being a good actor. I enjoy acting and would like to act in a film. I'd like to be remembered for being my own person and not copying anybody else.

MATTHEW

Lesson 3

The children recalled what they had learnt about Jesus from hearing and reading stories from the gospels and from learning about the origin of some Christian festivals. They were then asked to write their thoughts about Jesus.

I think Jesus left a memorial of care and love because he wanted us to be a little bit like him and care and love our family and neighbours. I think he also leaves a memorial of courage to speak what we think and to stand up for what we think is right. I also think he left a memorial to help so we could help others that help us. I think the last thing, was his thoughts because a lot of people wrote them down.

KERRY

I think Jesus is remembered as a kind person, helpful, thoughtful, wise. He stood up for what he believed and was a good friend. I think he was a good healer and a calm person because when he healed that man with leprosy Jesus told him not to tell anyone but the man still did, because he was so excited at being cured. I think Jesus was a good person, but I think he was barmy for wanting to be crucified.

LEE

The teacher asked:

Did Jesus want to be crucified or did he allow himself to be crucified?

Why?

I think Jesus left the greatest puzzle of all, whether his story is true or not. There is said to be proof about him, but I'm not so sure. He left wonder. Why was he sent down here or was he just a wacko with strange and wonderful powers? He gave us different thoughts about God. Even though he was strange he was loving and kind. His powers were great and he left us with healed people.

ROWENA

A few weeks later Rowena died. The teacher helped the class, who were very upset, by recalling the work they had done on memorials and suggested they each wrote their own memorial about Rowena. These were put together in a book and sent to her parents. A memorial indeed!

The Easter Story through Clay

Possible Learning Outcomes

This work is designed to help children to:

- express feelings as well as knowledge and beliefs (AT1 and 2);
- to explore their own feelings about incidents in the Holy Week and Easter stories (AT2).

The children recalled the main events of Holy Week and were then allowed to choose which one they wished to represent in clay.

Praying in Gethsemane – Jesus is arrested

Crucifixion – Taken from the Cross

The Empty Tomb

This lesson became an RE lesson only when the children shared what they had done with the whole class, and explained why they had chosen a particular event, and were ready to try and answer any questions the other children raised.

Easter through Art

9–10 year olds

Possible Learning Outcomes

This is a most useful method for 9 and 10 year olds, by which age they can be expected to have a reasonable grasp of some of the Holy Week accounts. It provides an opportunity to help children to:

- consolidate what has been learned about Easter (AT1);
- reflect on what Christians believe (AT1/2).

The teacher began by asking:

What do detectives do?

'Yes, they look for clues,' the teacher continued. 'Today I want you to be detectives. You'll find all the clues in a picture. Detectives often work in pairs so they can discuss the clues, so I want you to work in pairs.'

The pictures were placed round the room. The children were asked to walk around and look carefully at each one, noticing as many details as possible. This was followed by class discussion based on:

What were the pictures about?

Why do you think they were painted?

Each pair chose a picture to study in detail, and recorded their answers to the following questions on a worksheet:

1. **Give your picture a really interesting title.**
2. **What do you think the artist is trying to say?**
3. **What do you find interesting about the picture?**
4. **Write down any questions you want to ask, or anything that puzzles you.**
5. **How would you want to draw a picture of this event? (Use another sheet of paper.)**

   or: Read the Bible account. Is the picture accurate?

These answers were then used in a follow-up discussion with the children sitting in a circle.

The pictures came from a variety of sources: photographs taken in churches; postcards from churches, cathedrals and art galleries; posters from art galleries, and pictures from magazines. The biblical reference was written on the back of each. All were mounted on thick card. If small pictures are being used, e.g. postcards, the children might be encouraged to use magnifying-glasses to assist them in their detection.

(For more-detailed work on using pictures see Cooling, M. *Jesus through Art, The Bible through Art* and *Art and Music Toolkit*, all available from RMEP. Children aged 9 and 10 years can be seen using pictures about Easter in the BBC Education video *Eggshells and Thunderbolts*, on teaching RE in primary schools.)

A mural in the Anglican cathedral at Muranga, Kenya. (Photograph reproduced by kind permission of Cynthia Chitsiga.)

Here are some 10 year olds' answers to the four questions on the worksheet:

1. Give your picture an interesting title.

Anger in the Temple

The unfair trial

Skull hill's sorrow

The risen Christ rules!

2. What do you think the artist is trying to say?

The disciples aren't particularly bothered.

[They were asleep in the Garden of Gethsemane. This kind of answer gives the teacher an opportunity to challenge it by asking: 'Could there have been another reason for them falling asleep?']

In this crucifixion the artist is trying to express the sorrow, and tragedy of Jesus's death.

The faces of the viewers are either scared, distressed or full of mourning.

The artist is saying that Jesus is suffering.

The artist is saying that his three friends still care. [Pietà.]

The artist is saying that Jesus is still mighty.

3. What interested you?

The colours aren't as bold as in a modern picture.

We found it interesting the way there was lightness behind where Jesus was.

We found it interesting that there were so many details in the picture.

4. Are there any questions you want to ask ...?

Where is Gethsemane?

Why was Jesus praying?

Why did Judas betray Jesus?

Why hasn't Jesus got a halo when the disciples have?

Why is Jesus nailed and the other two are tied?

Why is Jesus wearing a crown of thorns and the robbers aren't?

Why are most of the people wearing red? Is it a sign of blood?

Why is there a soldier waiting at the crucifixion?

Was it his family taking him off the cross?

Why did Jesus let himself be killed?

Only a few of the questions children wanted to ask required a factual answer. In many instances the teacher directed the question back to the children by asking:

What do you think the answer might be?

Why?

The lesson ended with the children working out the sequence of events with the pictures that had been used, and then trying to insert the pictures that hadn't been chosen by anyone.

Possible Follow-Up Work

This work could be followed up by asking:

What are people willing to die for today?

and/or

What are people willing to suffer for today?

Is there anything so important to us that we would be prepared to suffer for it?

The Easter Story Expressed through Poetry

9–10 year olds

Possible Learning Outcomes

This work is designed to help children to:

- consolidate what they have learnt about the events of Holy Week and identify the key aspects of each event (AT1);
- identify the key aspects in an important event in their own lives (AT2).

The children recapped what they had learnt about the events of Holy Week. As this was being done the teacher listed the key words on the board. The children were then asked to describe one of the events in poetic form using the minimum of words, so that each word needed to be chosen with care.

The model used was: line 1 – one word; line 2 – two words; and so on, with the last line containing only one word.

Jerusalem
Jesus Christ
Be our King!
Waving of palm leaves
Hosanna!

Mockery
False witness
Crown of thorns
Place of the skull
Crucified

Court
False witness
Pleasing the crowd
Mocking 'King of Jews'
Crucifixion

Walking
Emmaus road
Talking with stranger
Telling him about himself
Jesus alive!

The children were encouraged to write out their poem on a background whose colour reflected the mood of the poem.

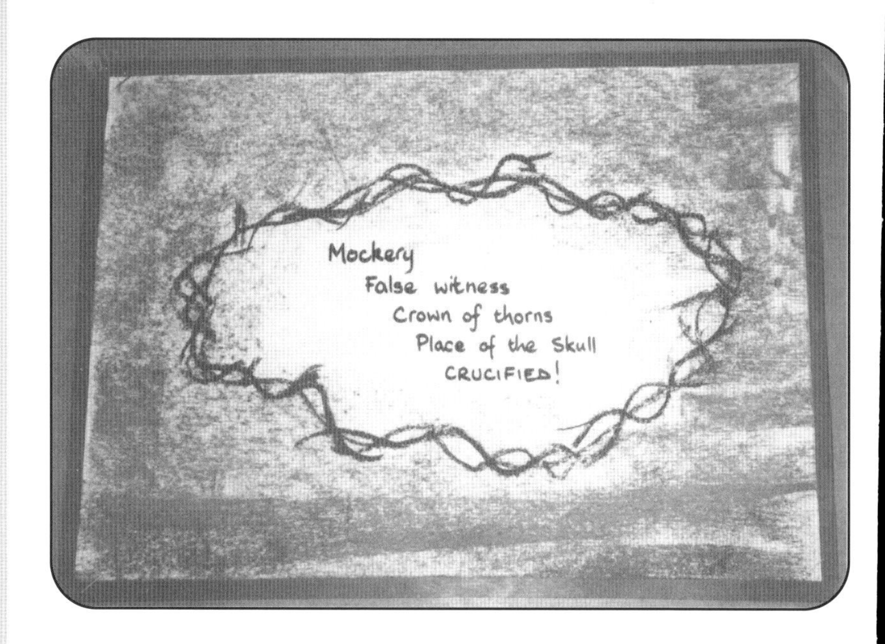

Possible Follow-Up Work

The children could be asked to think of an important occasion in their own lives, to identify the key aspects of this occasion in their own lives and to use these in poetic form, as above.

Reflecting on Holy Week through Music and Art

Possible Learning Outcomes

This work is designed to help children to:

- reflect on their own feelings (AT2);
- reflect on the possible feelings aroused by the events of Holy Week (AT1/2).

For this lesson the teacher recorded three one-minute extracts of music of different mood and tempo.

The teacher played the first minute, asking the children to be aware how the music made them feel, and to recall a time when they felt like that. When the music ended she asked them to choose two colours of pastels which reflected their feelings.

When the children had chosen their pastels and a sheet of coloured sugar paper, the teacher explained that she would repeat the one minute of music and that during that one minute they could express their feeling in an abstract, non-representational form. If they wished they could do it with their eyes closed and/or a pastel in each hand. Any method was acceptable. As soon as the music stopped the children were asked to stop, to look quietly at their pictures and recall their feelings.

The children held up their work for others to see and were invited to say something about their pictures, but there was no pressure to do so. It was clearly understood that no one else was allowed to comment.

The class was asked to recall five or six of the main events of Holy Week, such as:

> Palm Sunday, The Last Supper, The Arrest in the Garden, The Crucifixion, The Resurrection.

These events were listed on the board.

The children were told that they would now hear another minute of music. They were asked to look at the list of events on the board as they listened and to decide which one best fitted the music.

Again, using two colours of pastels they coloured their paper in an abstract manner whilst the music was replayed. The children shared their pictures and were invited to comment on the feelings they had expressed. After sharing, a third piece of music of a contrasting type was played, and the same procedure was followed.

It was interesting to note that for any one piece of music children chose different events, and had very good reasons for doing so. This approach produced a very reflective atmosphere and the children entered into some of the feelings evoked by the events.

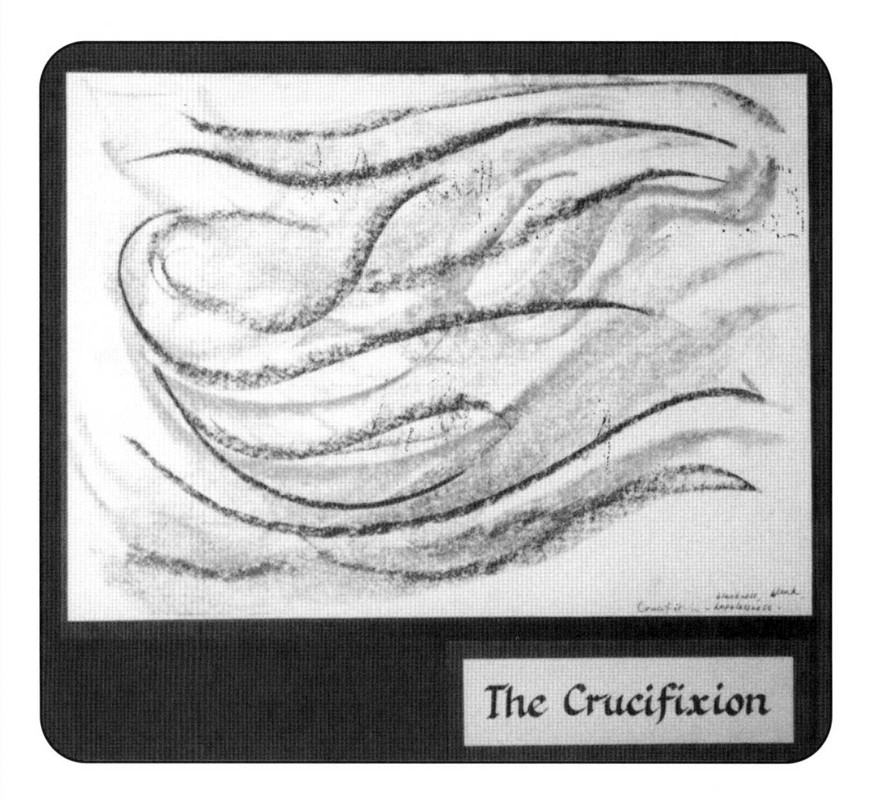

The Crucifixion